More of

YESTERDAY'S TUCSON TODAY

TUBAC • TUMACACORI • NOGALES

YOUR GUIDE TO WALKING THE HISTORIC TOWNS OF THE SANTA CRUZ VALLEY

Book 2

Harry and Mary Cuming

First Edition Published 1996 by
Trillium Enterprises
Tucson, Arizona
*

1st Printing December 1996

* Dedicated with love to our grandchildren*
ALLISON CUMING
CHRISTOPHER CUMING

Printed by
WEST PRESS
Tucson, Arizona

Library of Congress Catalog Card Number: 96-90642

Cuming, Harry and Mary
More of Yesterday's Tucson Today Tubac • Tumacacori • Nogales
Your Guide to Walking the Historic Towns of the Santa Cruz Valley
142 p.
ISBN 0-9653649-2-5
Printed in the United States of America

Contents

Introduction

This new book contains 92 buildings and sites from Tucson, south to Nogales.

The book covers seven historic districts and sites:

Fort Lowell Historic District
University and University West Historic District
Armory Park Historic District
West of the Santa Cruz
Miscellaneous Sites
Tubac and Tumacacori Mission
Nogales

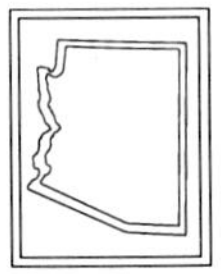

This plaque design has been placed on some historic buildings and sites by the Tucson - Pima County Historical Commission and the Arizona Historical Society, the Tubac Historical Society and the Pimeria Alta Historical Society.

The sketches have been taken from THE AUTHOR'S SKETCH BOOK intended to be used for watercolor paintings of historic buildings. The stories accompanying the sketches are, for the most part, taken from newspaper clippings found in the files at the libraries of the Arizona Historical Society Museum, the Tubac Historical Society and the Pimeria Alta Historical Society Museum.

Maps are not to scale and are the artist's rendition and are included at the beginning of each historic district. Your walk can be followed in numbered sequence. In the miscellaneous section each building has its own map.

Santa Cruz County was created in 1899 with Nogales being the county seat and the major port of entry into Arizona from Mexico. Santa Cruz County is named after the river flowing through it. It is very historic as the Spanish explorers and missionaries were the earliest visitors to travel this part of the country, Father Kino in 1691, and the founding of the Tubac Presidio in 1752. Many Americans heading for the west coast, during the California Gold Rush of 1849, left their mark.

Enjoy your walks, they will be good for you!!

1928 — Mary Cuming — 1996

I wish to thank my wife Mary for all the support and forbearance in encouraging me to pursue my art hobby.

Without Mary's continuous effort and unselfish help this work would never have been completed.

Tucson

The Founding of Tucson

1768: Father Garces was in charge of the Mission San Xavier Del Bac and frequently stayed with the Pima Indians in their village, located on the west side of the Santa Cruz River at the base of Sentinel Peak ("A" Mountain). The Pimas' name for their village was Schuk shon, meaning the place at the foot of Black Mountain. The Spanish called it San Agustin del Tucson.

1770: Captain Anza, who was the commander of the Tubac Presidio ordered a wall, with gunports and lookout tower, to be built in the middle of this Pima village as protection against the Apaches.

1775: Colonel Don Hugo O'Conor, an Irishman, joined the Spanish army and was appointed Chief Inspector of the northern Spanish defenses in America. O'Conor met Father Garces at San Xavier Del Bac and together they came to the east bank of the Santa Cruz River across from the Pima village. They marked out, on August 20th, 1775, what would eventually become El Presidio Wall. O'Conor also closed down the Tubac Presidio which was constantly being raided by Apaches.

1775: Captain Allande, newly appointed as commander, arrived in Tucson and built a log palisade, and later built and paid for El Presidio's first chapel. A bridge over the Santa Cruz connected the new fort with the Pima village.

1782: Captain Allande, badly wounded in the leg and along with 20 soldiers, held off and saved the fort from the largest raid on Tucson by about 600 Apaches.

1783: Lieutenant Abate finished El Presidio wall in adobe bricks. This wall was about 12' high and 3' thick at the base.

1797: Tucson's population reaches 395 and the Mission Church San Xavier Del Bac was completed.

Tucson's Heritage

Tucson has a reputation of being one of the oldest documented settlements in the United States.

Tucson was the site of a prehistoric Hohokam village from about 450 A.D. - 1250 A.D. Today, Native Americans call the Tucson area their home. Among these are the Tohono O'Odham and Pima whom archaeologists believe may be descendants of the Hohokam. Excavations have discovered the homes of the historic Tohono O'Odham Indians. We have beautiful Spanish missions to prove the Spanish were here and the Mexican people have stayed to play their part as settlers and entrepreneurs. Anglo-American pioneers were relativly latecomers, arriving during the 19th and 20th centuries. They, also, have left their mark.

Spanish period	from 1775-1821
Mexican period	from 1821-1863
Arizona Territory	from 1863-1912
Arizona statehood	from 1912

Arizona was declared a territory by President Abraham Lincoln February 24, 1863, and on February 14, 1912, President Taft declared Arizona a state.

The author has tried to reveal this heritage and unique character of Tucson in sketch and text.

Introduction to Fort Lowell Historic District

Village of El Fuerte

Fort Lowell Historic District, which is less than 1/4 square mile in area, not only includes the fort property but also is the site of a Hohokam settlement. There are about 30 historic designated properties, some of which are found in the village of El Fuerte.

The Hohokam people had a large settlement on this site from about 300 A.D. to about 1250 A.D. Mexican ranchers, as well as Mormon families, settled in the area after the fort was closed in 1891 and the village of El Fuerte (The Fort) was formed.

The district has kept the rural and scenic appearance much like it was during its early cultural days. Native plants, rural and irregular roads, as well as informal and southwestern architectural-styled homes complement and blend into the historic district.

Map No. 1 Fort Lowell Historic District

Map Site No.

1. Cottonwood Lane
2. Post Hospital
3. Veterans Memorial and Flag Pole
4. Commanding Officer's Quarters
5. Officers Quarters
6. Fort Lowell
7. Chief Trumpeter
8. Headquarters Buildings (see A, B, C, D)
9. Pioneer Soldier Memorial
10. Quartermaster Depot and Post Trader (see A, B, C)
11. Cavalry Barracks and Band Barracks (see A, B, C)
12. Infantry Barracks and Laundresses' Quarters (see A, B)
13. Post Hospital (Post Surgeon)
14. Hohokam Site
15. Chapel of San Pedro
16. School

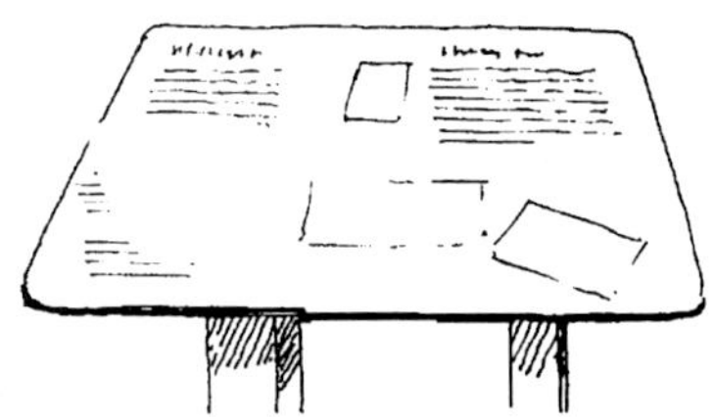

These interpretive signs are placed around the perimeter of the Fort Lowell Historic Parade Ground.
To start your tour, proceed west down the Cottonwood Tree Lane to the Fort Lowell Museum.
1995

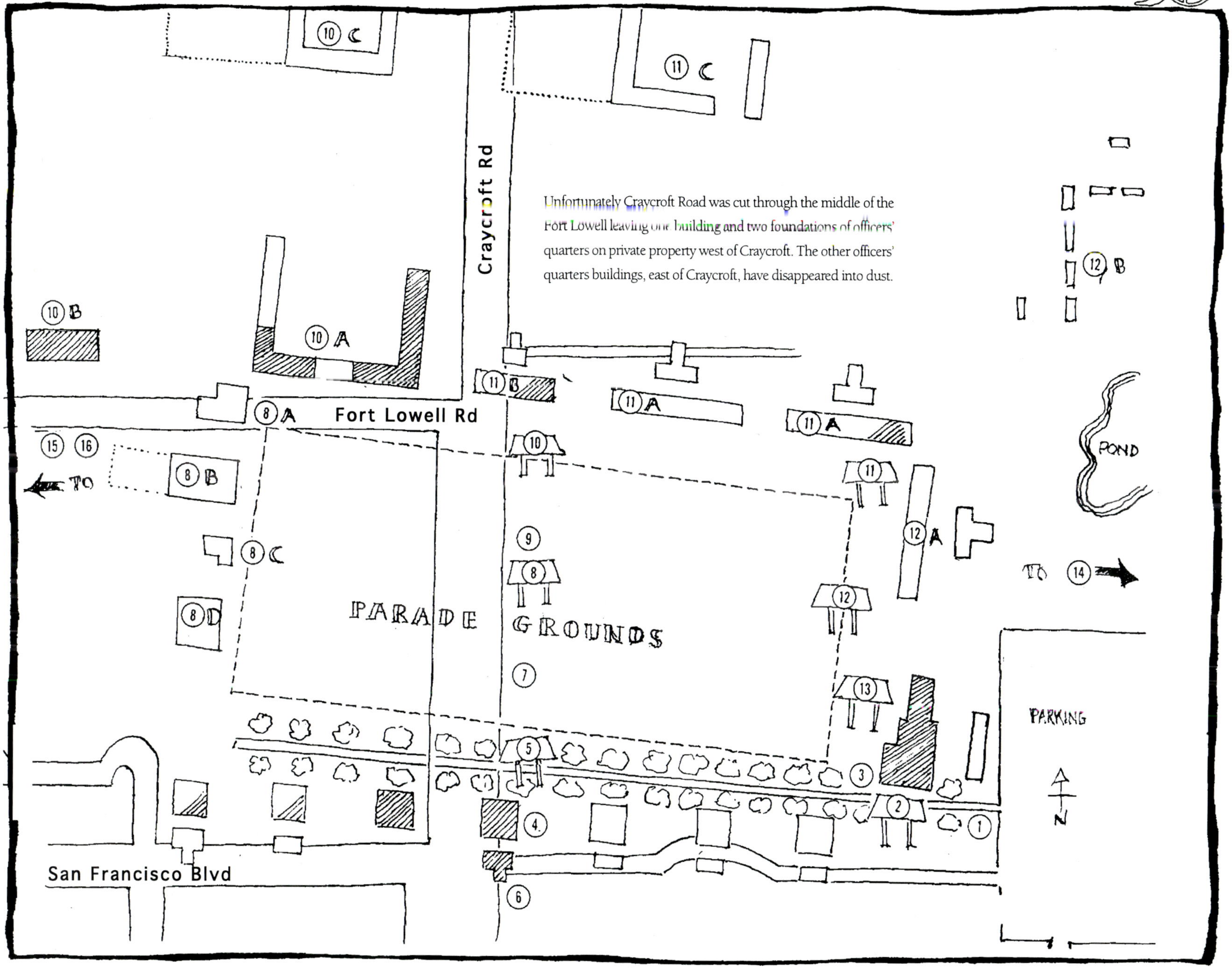

No. 1 Fort Lowell Historic District

Cottonwood Lane

1 Planted shortly after Fort Lowell was established in 1873. The trees were irrigated by acequias or open ditches with water diverted from Pantano Wash. The beautiful shade trees made Fort Lowell an oasis in an otherwise barren area. After the fort was abandoned in 1891 the trees died and were cut up for firewood. Now they have been replanted as they originally were in the heyday of Fort Lowell.

Presented by the Conservation Department of Tucson's Women's Club.
Mrs. H.M. Merritt 1964 - 65

Fort Lowell

The military post established in 1862 near downtown Tucson was moved to this location in 1873. One of the many active forts on the Arizona Frontier, Lowell also served as a major supply depot, influencing the economy and social life of the community. At its peak in the 1880s, three companies of infantry and two troops of cavalry - more than 250 officers and soldiers - were stationed here. The need for Fort Lowell steadily declined after Geronimo's surrender in 1886 and despite local protest it was closed by the army in 1891.

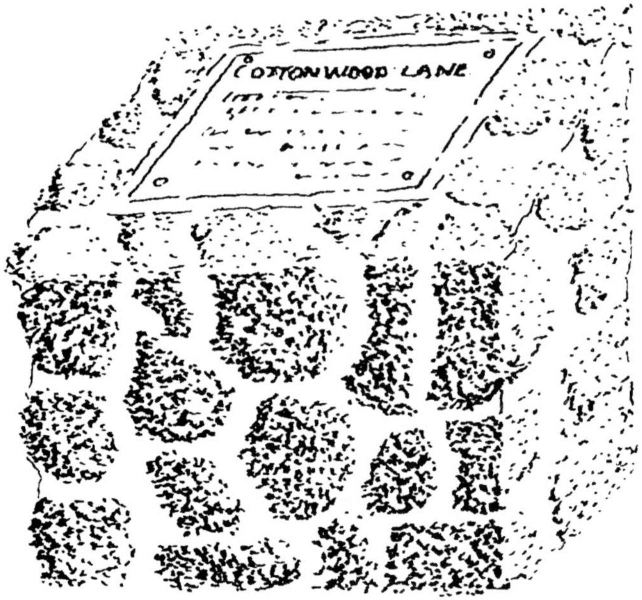

Fort Lowell was named after Charles R. Lowell, U.S.A. 6th Cavalry, who was killed in Virginia during the Civil War.

Author's Note: There is a discrepancy between the original A.H.S. sign and the newer one posted in 1996 so we show them both.

Cottonwood Lane looking west with Officers' Row on left and parade grounds behind wooden fence on right, 1888.

2

Post Hospital

The Fort Lowell Hospital had 13 rooms and accommodated 16 beds. The building was 60 feet wide and 120 feet long. The facility also contained an isolation ward, a surgeon's office, a dispensary, storerooms, a wash room, morgue, and quarters for the enlisted men on the hospital staff. Fireplaces heated the building in winter. In summer the long hallways encouraged breezes, and shutters, porches, and cottonwood trees shaded it. By the 1880s, a tin roof reduced leaks; plaster and white paint adorned the walls; and wood floors replaced dirt. Behind the hospital, to the east, sat a 20- by 78-foot kitchen building.

Fort Lowell 1873-1891

The army originally established Camp Lowell in 1866 on the outskirts of Tucson. Because of unsanitary conditions there, in 1873 the army moved the post here, 7 miles northeast of Tucson. Fort Lowell, so designated in 1879, boasted four companies of cavalry and infantry. It was one of 12 large military posts in Arizona territory during the last quarter of the 19th century, the final years of the Apache Wars. The fort closed in 1891. (3)

Tucson thanks the Boy Scouts of America for the protective roof over the remains of the Post Hospital. It was installed in 1915 and has prevented further deterioration of this old adobe building.

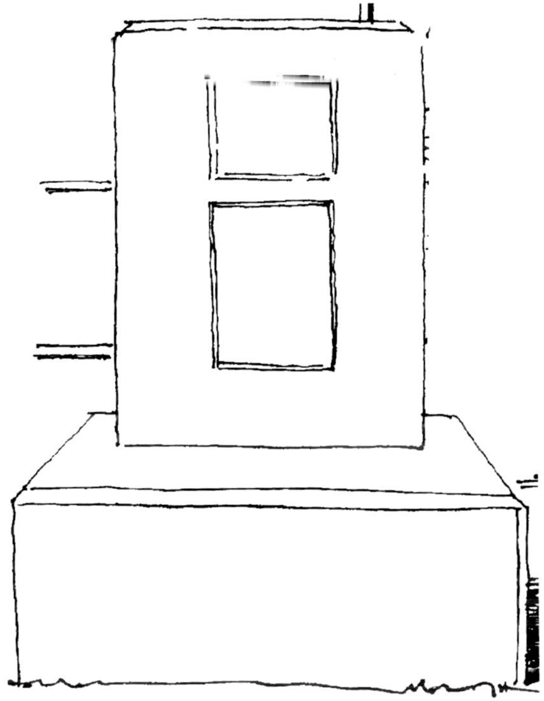

Flag Pole

In memory
of
State Senator
James W. Ewing
6 - 12 - 1891 -- 6 - 25 - 1953
President Catalina Council
Boy Scouts of America
1952-1953

Veterans Memorial
Fort Lowell Park

Dedicated to the enduring memory of the men and women who faithfully served in the military forces of the United States of America and in grateful acknowledgment of their contribution to this nation which, in time of peril, found in them its protection.

Veterans Affairs Committee City of Tucson 1979.

Erected May, 1958
by Pima County
Board of Supervisors
in Co-operation with
The U.S. Bureau of Public Records

Commanding Officer's Quarters

4

These buildings, built in 1963 northeast of the original, are a reconstruction of the commander's quarters and now a museum under the direction of the Arizona Historical Society. The building, including the ocotillo fence, are authentically reproduced from early photographs and documents from the fort's active years. The mantas (cotton ceilings) inside as well as the shutters and canales (drains) outside are all faithfully reproduced.

This building was originally built in the center of the south end of the parade ground. It was 42-by 42-foot, divided into four equal rooms. Two wide hallways bisected the building. At the rear of the quarters was a detached building which contained a kitchen, dining room, one room for servants, and a pantry. A root cellar was constructed under part of the main building.

Officers' Quarters

Private Residence

5

The officers of Fort Lowell and their families lived in 7 adobe homes – Officers' Row. During peak periods of military activity, up to three families lived in each building. After 1889 two smaller houses for married noncommissioned officers were added to the east end of the row.

Each 42- by 42-foot structure had a dirt floor, adobe walls, and, after mid-1880s, redwood floors, plastered interiors, shutters, and porches with ocotillo fences. An 18- by 35-foot kitchen lay to the rear, with a pantry, kitchen, and dining room and servants' room. A walled yard enclosed each individual compound, along with a garden for food.

The army officially considered women and children mere camp followers and made little provision for them. Nonetheless, the families provided warmth and stability and they endured the hardships of frontier military life with their husbands and fathers.

The remains of the three officers quarters, west of the original location of the commanding officer's quarters, are visible. A Mrs. Dolly Cates bought the property containing these officer's quarters in 1900 and established "Mrs Cates" T.B. Sanatorium. She ran it until 1928 when the present owners bought the property. Two of the buildings were gutted by fire in 1970 and are in ruins. The third building is being occupied as a residence at the time of the publication of this book.

6

Fort Lowell

Largest of the early Arizona military installations

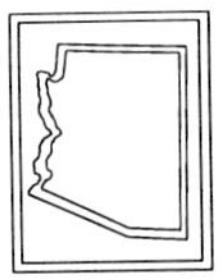

This was the supply base for military posts in Southern Arizona during the long warfare against the Apaches. Built in 1873, it was Gen. Nelson A. Miles' headquarters in the final campaign against Geronimo, and was abandoned in 1891.

Presented by Head Camp

7

Chief Trumpeter

This 12-foot statue, by local artist Dan Bates, was erected in the park in 1991. The detail of the uniform and equipment is accurate for the U.S. Army of the 1880s. The Chief Trumpeter was a noncommissioned officer. Bates donated his time sculpting the work. A local foundry cast the statue and local money supported the monument so there was no expense for the taxpayer.

Headquarters Buildings

Quartermaster and Commissary Office

(8)

A The administrative center was located in a 40- by 40-foot building, now gone, the site buried under present day Fort Lowell Road. Here the quartermaster and commissary officers, sergeants, and clerks directed the supplying and feeding of the troops at Fort Lowell and across southern Arizona.

Guardhouse

B The guardhouse was a 50- by 50-foot adobe and stone building with rooms for the officer and sergeant of the guard, a general prisoner's room, a tool room, and 7 cells only 4- by 7-feet wide. In the rear were a 30- by 50-foot exercise yard and 2 privies.

The army enforced strict military disciplines at Fort Lowell. The soldiers' typical offences included theft, desertion, absence without leave, insubordination, swearing, and drunkenness. Court-martials determined guilt and punishment. During the hottest months, the post commander occasionally tried to send prisoners to Alcatraz, off the California Coast, because the Fort Lowell guardhouse was too crowded.

Bakery

C Every soldier stationed at Fort Lowell received 22 ounces of bread as part of his daily ration. The baker produced the loaves at the post bakery, a 32- by 30-foot building with one oven. The baker was an enlisted man who received an extra 40 cents per day over and above his regular pay of $13.00 a month. He was excused from all other military duties.

Post Commander and Post Adjutant's Office

D The nerve center of Fort Lowell was this 56- by 56-foot adobe building. The post commander and post adjutant made their offices here. When the regimental commander and his staff were on post, they lived in the building. It contained a room for court-martials and a library with books, newspapers, and magazines for the soldiers.

(8) A

Quartermaster and Commissary Office

(8) B

Guardhouse

(8) C

Bakery

(8) D

Post Commander and Post Adjutant's Office

(9)

Pioneer Soldier Memorial

Lest we forget those rugged pioneer soldiers who tamed the west this memorial is erected to perpetually remind us of their service

Erected this 30th day of May 1965
by Morgan McDermott
Post No.7 The American Legion
Department of Arizona

Quartermaster Depot and Post Trader

Private Residence

These buildings are still in existence today and are found across Craycroft Road on the north side of Fort Lowell Road. (10) The quartermaster and commissary building (10A) is at the corner and the Post Trader's building (10B) is the third building along Fort Lowell Road.

A Fort Lowell was a major supply depot for forts around southern Arizona territory. The quartermaster and commissary depot is on private property directly west, across Craycroft Road and north of Fort Lowell Road. The quartermaster department supplied all military clothing, camp and garrison equipment, wagons, draft animals, forage, fuel, and materials for construction and repair. The U-shaped building, the largest on the post, had over 9,300 square feet of floor and cellar space. The commissary department stored food here. Troopers supplemented the army ration with produce they grew in the gardens on the post. The ordinance department used the depot for storing weapons, ammunition, cartridge belts and boxes, and saddles.

C North of the depot were the 140- by 290-foot corrals, the stables, and the hay yard for the quartermaster's horses and mules. A quartermaster and commissary storehouse was constructed in 1893. The storehouse was U-shaped with 12-foot walls. A cellar, for the commissary supplies, was dug under the northwest wing to a depth of 15 feet. All that remains of the northwest portion of the building is the hole for the cellar. The rest of the building was turned into apartments in 1934.

Post Trader or Sutler's Store

Private Residence

In 1873 John B. "Pie" Allen built a trading post near Fort Lowell. The building is located on private property west of Craycroft Road and north of Fort Lowell Road, west of the commissary depot. Allen soon sold the store to Fred Austin. The 19 room structure contained storerooms, a bar, gaming rooms for officers and enlisted men, and living quarters. The post trader provided necessary and welcome diversions for the soldiers, but the establishment was a continual source of problems for Fort Lowell's commander. The army reprimanded Austin for keeping the bar open after hours, purveying whiskey, exceeding the set price of 30 cents a quart for beer, and selling more than the allowed three bottles of beer per man per day. The store closed in 1889.

10

B

In 1900 the old store was used as a sanitorium and later was converted to a hog farm. By 1934, the building was in ruins and a year later remodeling of the store began. The outside was plastered and the connecting archway was enclosed. In 1942, additional rooms were added.

Further restoration was done in 1973. The west wall, that connected the store to the stable area, was destroyed. The west wall of the chicken coop remains as it was incorporated into the west wall of a residence built in the late 1930s.

Cavalry Barracks and Band Barracks

From here west to the intersection of Craycroft and Fort Lowell Roads stood 2 cavalry barracks, 20- by 145-feet, and
1 band barrack, 20- by 92-feet. The 21 troops of the 2nd, 4th, 5th, and 6th cavalry regiments lived here. The band
(11) A barracks housed the Regimental bands when they were posted at Fort Lowell with the Regimental staffs. When the
musicians were not in residence, the quartermaster often used their barracks for storage.

B In 1889, when the army abolished the post trader's position, it set aside three rooms of the band barracks as a canteen. The army sold beer, wine, cider, soda, cigars, pies, sandwiches, and playing cards. They also provided such diversions as billiards, checkers, cards, and chess.

The kitchens sat to the north of the cavalry and band barracks. Each troop and regimental band prepared its own food in its own kitchen, and served meals in its own mess in the same building. Army rations consisted of pork, bacon, beef, bread, beans, peas, rice, coffee, potatoes, molasses, and canned goods.

C North of the cavalry barracks were covered stables and corrals for the cavalry units. The complex included hay yards, tool rooms, and a blacksmith shop.

In the northwest corner of the park there are a few adobe blocks and stones, all that remains of the regimental band barracks. When the fort closed this was used as a family home. The regimental band played every afternoon at 5 P.M. and Tucsonans would take a long wagon ride to hear the concert.

Infantry Barracks

The infantry barracks (no longer in existence) were 75 feet north of the hospital. The one-story building, like all the barracks at Fort Lowell, had walls 20 inches thick, a dirt roof, and a wooden porch. The barracks were 20 feet wide and 145 feet long, with a 20- by 50-foot kitchen building out back. A (12)

From 1873 to 1886, 11 companies of infantry were stationed here, with one or two companies usually on duty. They protected ranches and railroads, provided escorts, and watched waterholes for Apaches resisting confinement on the reservation. The infantryman was less mobile and less expensive to maintain than his counterpart in the cavalry. He rarely saw combat in Arizona territory.

Laundresses' Quarters

The laundresses' quarters, at Fort Lowell, sat northeast of the infantry barracks. They consisted of 8 adobe structures, each of which had two 15- by 15-foot rooms. B

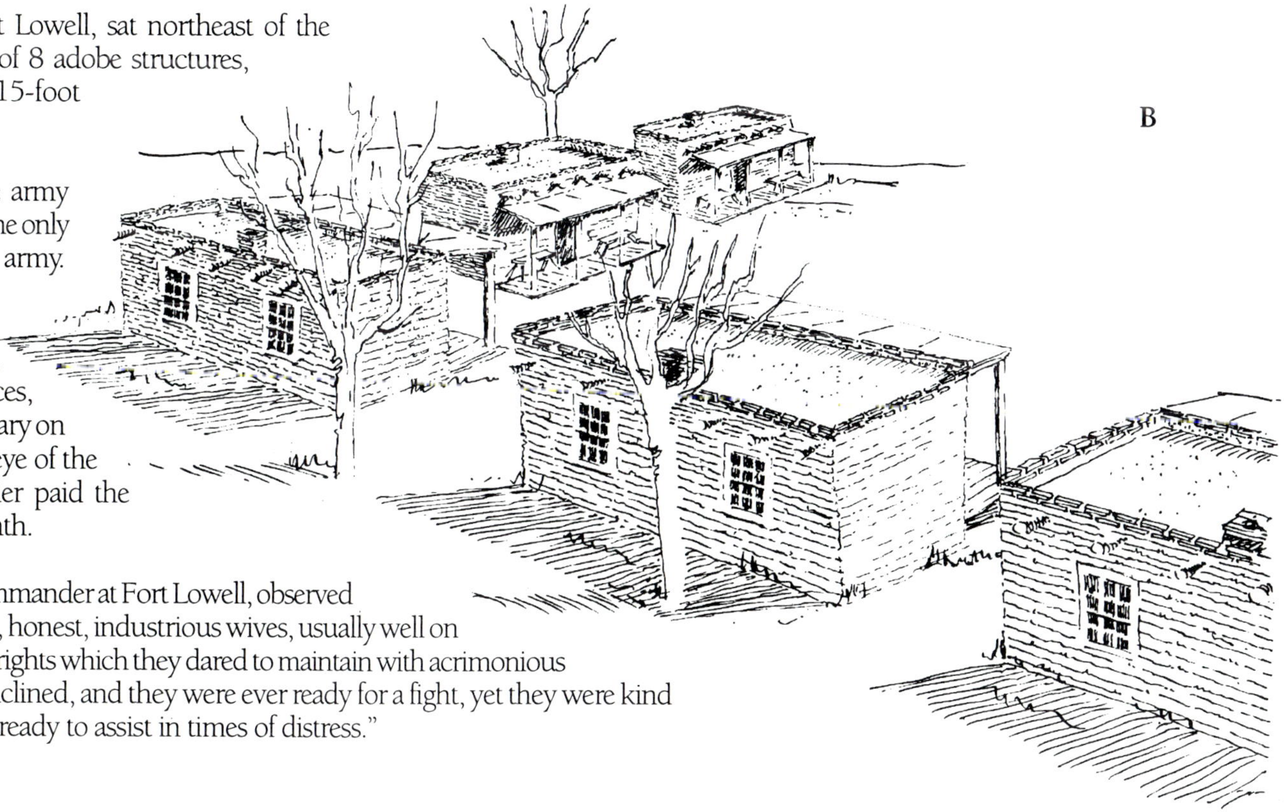

From 1803 until 1883, when the army phased them out, laundresses were the only women with official status in the army. Commanders appointed four laundresses from each company and furnished them with rations, fuel, transportation, medical services, and housing. They received their salary on payday when, under the watchful eye of the company commander, every soldier paid the women from $1.00 to $1.50 a month.

Lt. Col. George A. Forsyth, a post commander at Fort Lowell, observed of the laundresses, "They were good, honest, industrious wives, usually well on in years, minutely familiar with their rights which they dared to maintain with acrimonious volubility, as became the martially inclined, and they were ever ready for a fight, yet they were kind of heart if rough in manner, always ready to assist in times of distress."

Post Hospital

Post Surgeon

(13) The post surgeon was the cornerstone of army medical care. He was either a medical officer or a local civilian. At Fort Lowell 21 men served in this capacity, assisted by enlisted hospital stewards. The surgeon maintained the health of all military personnel, including wives, children, and civilian employees. He also regulated sanitation. He had no one else to consult, relying solely on his education, experience, and medical books.

By the 1870s, the post surgeon used antiseptics. A decade later, he had such anesthetics as sulfuric ether or chloroform. The soldiers' ailments commonly included malaria, diarrhea, venereal diseases, alcoholism, rheumatism, headaches, sprains, and gunshot wounds. Major Joseph R. Girard was post surgeon six different times from 1873-1891.

From an 1889 Photo

Hohokam Pit House

Hardy Site

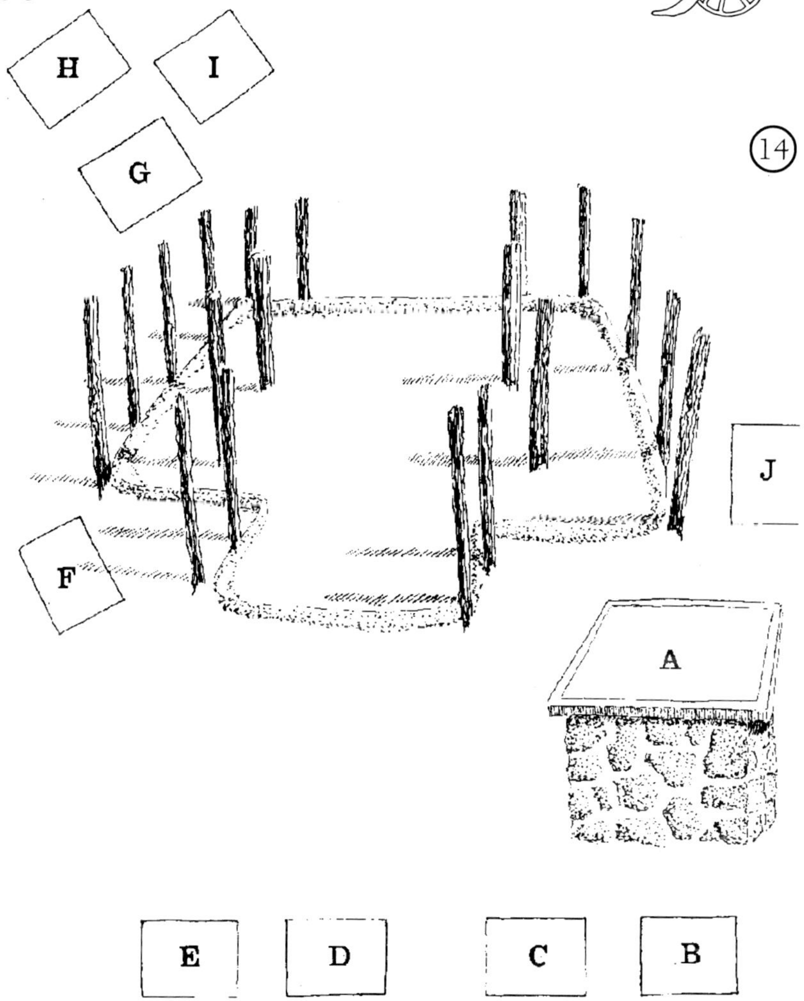

Hohokam

A. Inside a Hohokam House

B. Pima and Papago Liveway

C. Archaeology

D. The Tucson Basin A.D. 1150

E. The Tucson Basin in 1875

F. Trash Mound

G. Construction of a Pit House

H. The Village and its Environment

I. Outdoor Activities

J. Appearance of the Hohokam and Cremation

The Hardy Site, named after John Hardy the property owner, was excavated by volunteers from the Arizona State Museum from February, 1976 to July, 1978. The objective was to provide the Tucson area public and visitors to southern Arizona with an awareness of Tucson basin prehistory, especially that of the Hohokam culture.

Although this interpretive exhibit is almost 20 years old, it still is possible to read and understand the sketches explaining the Hohokam culture. We understand this outdoor exhibit will one day have new signage similar to the new 1995 signs now on the Fort Lowell parade ground.

(15)

Chapel of San Pedro at Fort Lowell

A tiny chapel built here in 1915 served the Barriada Del Rillito, a community now called El Fuerte. The fifteen immigrant Mexican families of this village gathered outside under mesquite trees to hear mass. In 1917 Senora Josefa De Mule donated land for a larger building. The second chapel, Santo Angel De La Guarda, was destroyed by a tornado in 1929. The present structure, also built by the men of El Fuerte, was dedicated in 1932.

Carmelite fathers from Tucson's Holy Family Church served the congregation until 1948, when St. Cyril's replaced this chapel as the neighborhood parish church.

Fort Lowell School

In 1908 El Fuerte had grown large enough and needed a school for the children. A dairy farmer, Mr. Jordan, donated the land and Mr. J. Knox Corbett paid for and supplied the building materials. (16)

Originally the school had two rooms, one for first to fourth grade and one for fifth through eighth grade. Average attendance was about 50 students, 25 per classroom. Spanish was not allowed in the classroom or schoolyard. By 1913, the school needed more room and used the Union Church next door as an annex.

In 1929 a new school, on Pima Avenue, was completed and the children carried all the furniture, books, etc. from the old adobe school which at various times became a dance hall, bar, store, and a chicken farm. All that remains now are the remnants of the adobe walls.

Introduction to the University and the West University Historic District

The West University Historic District, situated between the University of Arizona and downtown Tucson, was an upscale residential area. Although the U of A is not included in the city's historic district, we have included some of their National Historic Registered buildings in our book. We have included a note on 4th Avenue, the main route of the trolley and, later, the bus service from downtown Tucson to the U of A.

Map No. 2 University & West University Historic District

Map site No.

1. Arizona Historical Society Museum
2. University Street Car Line
3. Arizona State Museum
4. Anthropology Building
5. Old Main
6. Cannon-Douglass Residence
7. George E.P. Smith Residence
8. Y.W.C.A.
9. Rondstadt House (Private Residence)
10. 4th Avenue
11. Coronado Hotel

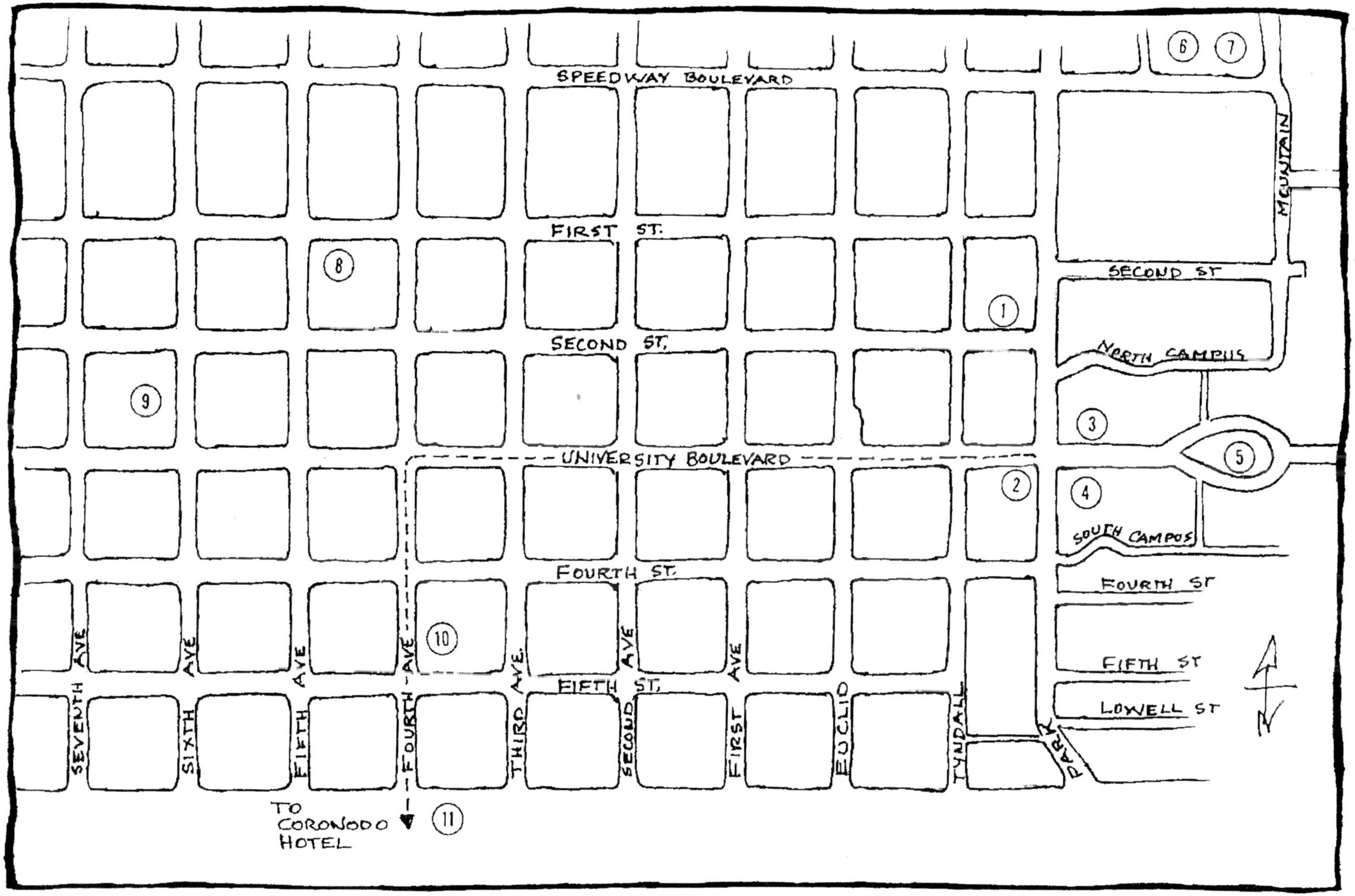

Map #2 University and West University Historic District

The Arizona Historical Society Museum

Wall Plaque

(1) This cross was a featured ornament above the entrance to Arizona's first Roman Catholic cathedral, dedicated to St. Augustine. The cathedral was constructed between 1863 and 1869 in Tucson, then the territorial capital. In 1883 Jules Leflein, a master stonemason, was commissioned to decorate the plain adobe entranceway of the cathedral. The massive stone facade, arched portal rose window, pediment, and this cross were the results of LaFlein's efforts. When the cathedral was demolished in 1936, George W. Chambers saved the stonework. In 1975 he donated these pieces to the Society. Where the facade was reconstructed and incorporated into the entryway of this building.

It is reported that George Chambers paid $75.00 for the arch, frame, and rose window and incorporated part of this into his home.

Woodmen of the World Memorial

Dum Taget Clamat

Jules Flin
N.E. Enfrance
Le 27, Feve 1847
Mort Le 19, Jan. 1915

Interesting headstone erected over the grave of Jules Leflein, a master stonemason honored with a "Woodmen of the World" Memorial in Holy Hope Cemetery - Tucson.

MUSEUM

University Street Car Line

2 Across from the main gate, on May 12, 1898, Charles F. Hoff, manager of the Tucson Street Railway Company, drove the final spike completing tracks to the downtown business district and residential areas further south. Mule-drawn street cars travelled a five-mile route along Third Street (University Boulevard) and Stone Avenue; the fare was a nickel. On June 1, 1906, the Tucson Rapid Transit Company inaugurated an electric street car system which played a significant role in residential development west of the University. A transportation era ended for Tucson when motor buses replaced the street cars after their last run December 31, 1930.

After ten years of hard work by volunteers, "Old Pueblo" trolley #10 ran again in April, '93. Any original Tucson streetcars have long disappeared into dust, but Car #10 is similar to the one-man cars that were in operation in Tucson during the 1915-1930 period.

Car #10 was leased from California and originally used on the Pacific Electric Line from Pasadena to Los Angeles. It has also been a movie star, used in such movies as the M.G.M. production of *"Singin' in the Rain"*, starring Gene Kelly. It was returned to California in 1996.

In 1996, Old Pueblo Trolley, Inc., a nonprofit corporation of volunteers, purchased a street car, #4608, from the TTC (Toronto Transit Commission) in Toronto, Canada, and expect it to be running here in early 1997.

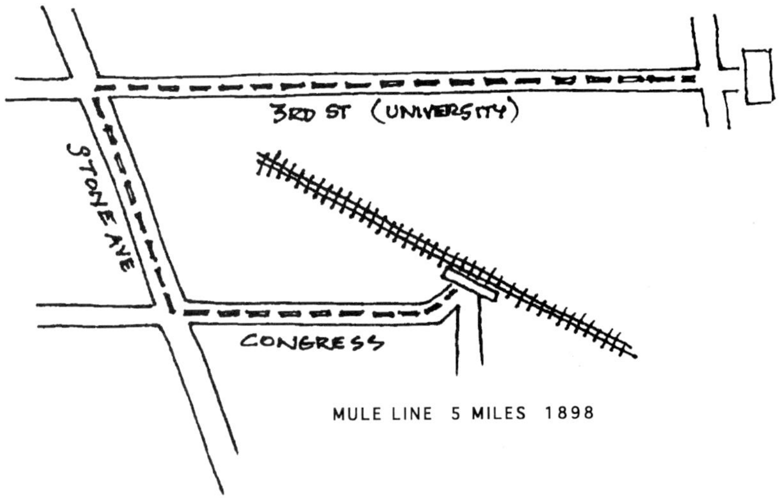

MULE LINE 5 MILES 1898

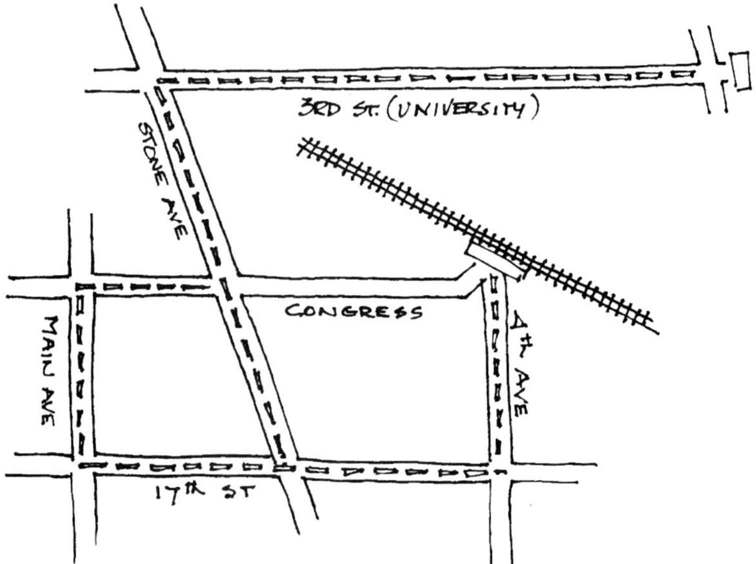

ELECTRIC LINE 1906

MULE LINE 1898-1906

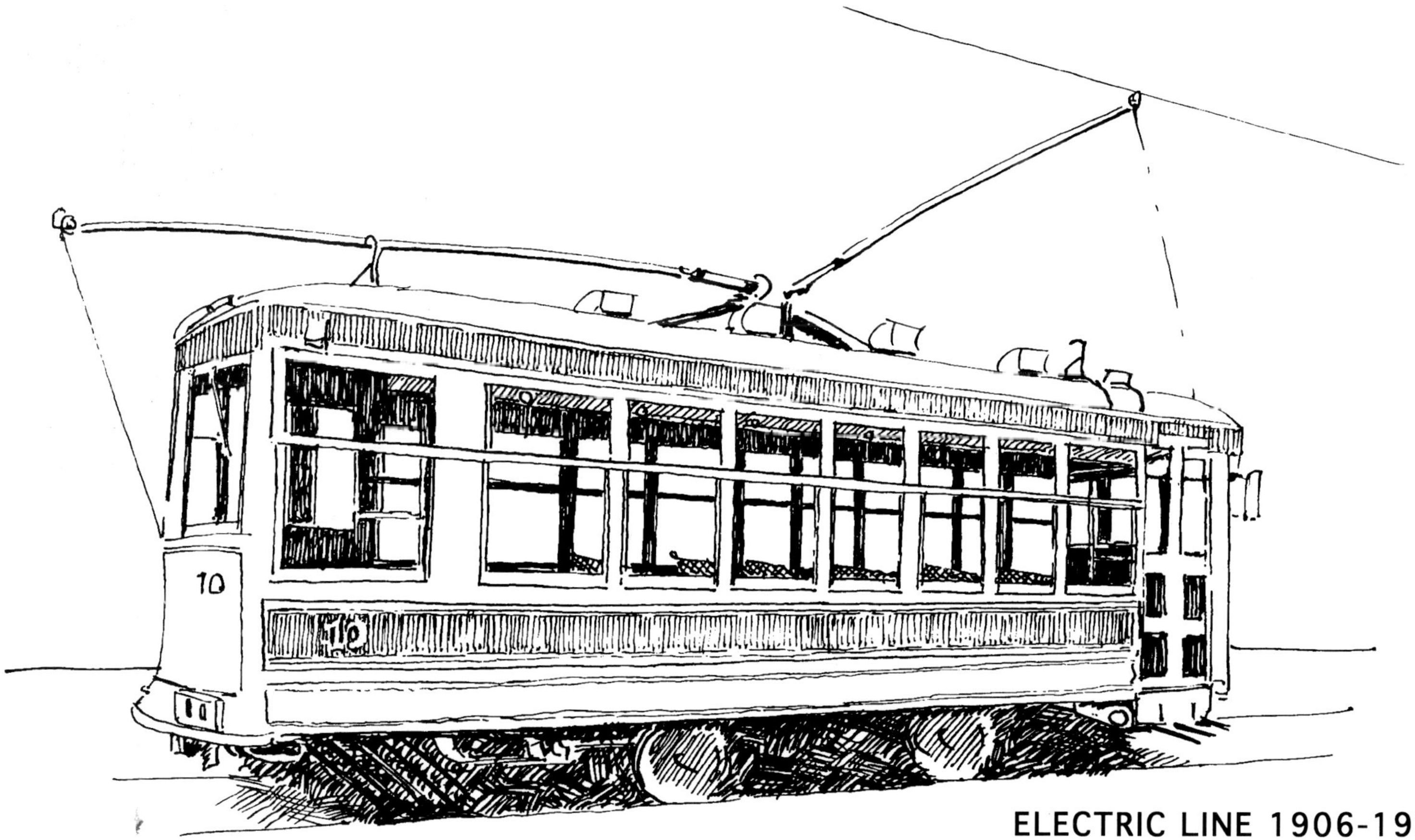

ELECTRIC LINE 1906-1930

Arizona State Museum

North Building

(3) This north building was built between 1923-1927. The impressive main lobby is marble-walled and includes a large staircase leading to the historic library on the second floor. On the left is a very impressive Native American display called "Paths of Life". The lifelike faces have been molded from actual Native Americans.

This building was originally built as the main university library and held special Arizona collections on mining, agriculture, and law. It was replaced by the new main library on campus in 1976. This building then became adapted as the Arizona State Museum, North Building.

Anthropology Building or Arizona State Museum

South Building

④

This building started as the Arizona State Museum and these south and north buildings are listed on the National Register of Historic Places.

In 1893, the Learning Center for Study of Southwestern Anthropology was created. Displays on the life of native peoples of the Southwest, as well as their crafts and animal life, are on display on the second floor.

Old Main

(5) On March 12, 1885, Governor Frederick A. Tritle signed legislation creating the University of Arizona. Selim M. Franklin and C.C. Stephens, Pima delegates to the 13th Territorial Legislature, fathered this bill. Jacob S. Mansfeld solicited the 40-acre site from William S. Read, E.B. Gifford and Ben C. Parker. James M. Creighton was architect, M.J. Sullivan contractor. Groundbreaking was October 27, 1887. Classes started October 1, 1891, with 6 faculty, 6 freshmen and 26 preparatory students. "Old Main" is listed in the National Register of Historic Places.

The plaque doesn't mention that William S. Read was a saloon keeper and that E.B. Gifford and Ben C. Parker were professional gamblers.

The Alexander Berger Memorial

The fountain is erected with enduring affection in honor of (13) sons of the University of Arizona who answered their country's call for service and gave the last full measure of devotion in the World War of 1917-1918.

"The Right is more Precious than Peace."

Alexander Berger, from Virginia, spent the winters on his ranch in Vail. He financed this fountain, as well as giving $100,000 to build the Tucson Temple of Music and Art. He and his brother Harry were patrons of the arts. General John J. Pershing, Commander of the American Expeditionary Force in World War I, dedicated the fountain in front of "Old Main" in 1920.

CUMING

Cannon-Douglass Residence

6

Dr. William Austin Cannon had this house built during 1904-1905. He was the first resident botanist with the Carnegie Desert Laboratory in 1902 and worked there until 1926. Dr. Cannon sold the house in 1913 to Dr. Andrew Ellicott Douglass, an astronomer who in 1896 had located the site for the Lowell Observatory in Flagstaff. Dr. Douglass, founder of dendrochronology, also built the Steward Observatory at the University of Arizona. Due to his early leadership, the University of Arizona is one of the world's leaders in the sciences of astronomy and dendrochronology.

This is a typical "Arizona Style" bungalow. The foundations and portions of the walls are built of rock from "A" Mountain.

Dr. Cannon, his wife Jennie, an artist, and two sons, arrived in Tucson in 1903.

Note:
Dendrochronology is the study of dating the age of a tree by its annual rings formed during growth.

George E.P. Smith Residence

7

Dr. Smith built this house in 1904 in anticipation of his marriage to Maud North, a Tucson teacher. The house which he designed was the first building on the north side of Speedway. Dr. Smith was a University of Arizona Professor of engineering and physics from 1900-1906, of irrigation engineering from 1906-1955, and emeritus to 1975. He pioneered in measuring Arizona's ground water and brought recognition to the University as a center for the study of water use in arid lands.

George E.P. Smith said that although his father built the home in 1904, it was originally occupied by William H. Sawtelle, an attorney from Alabama, who moved to Tucson for his wife's health.

Sawtelle became a judge for the U.S. District Court of Arizona. He was nominated to the 9th Circuit Court of Appeals in San Francisco.

Dr. George Smith, with his wife and son, moved into the home in 1906. He taught at the University of Arizona from 1900-1955 and published 100 articles related to water issues. Dr. Smith died, aged 101, in March 1974.

YWCA

8

The Franklin family sold 3 lots to the "Y" in the 1920s. Mrs. Franklin gave a check for $500 back to the "Y" to start the building fund.

The YWCA was built in 1929. By 1987 the "Y" was in financial difficulties. Great Western Realty bought the building and leased it back to the "Y".

The YWCA was designed by architect Henry O. Jaastad who was the University West District's most prolific designer. Along with the YWCA, he designed over 50 residences and 5 churches in this district. The YWCA is a blend of Spanish colonial revival and pueblo styles.

The Ronstadt House

Private Residence

9

Fred Ronstadt was born Frederico Jose Maria Ronstadt, in 1868, near the Mexican town of Cananea, Sonora.

In 1882, he was sent to Tucson as an apprentice in a relative's carriage shop. By 1888, Fred had established his first business, a blacksmith and wagon shop, on south Meyer Street.

In 1900, he purchased a site on Broadway Blvd. from the city of Tucson, the first lot ever sold by the city. This site became the F. Ronstadt Hardware Company in 1901 and employed up to 65 men in the adjoining carriage factory. This site is now the location of the Sun Tran bus terminal.

By 1904, the automobile forced Ronstadt out of the buggy business and into selling the single-cylinder Oldsmobile car, and farm equipment.

Ronstadt had married Sara Levine, in the 1890s, and they had four children. Sara died of cholera in 1903 expecting their fifth child. In 1904 Fred married Lupe Dalton and built this house for his new bride.

Fred was an active musician and organized the Tucson Philharmonic Band which became Arizona's Regimental Band during the Spanish-American War.

Linda Ronstadt, the singer, continues her grandfather's love of music today. Linda, along with this "old house" and the Ronstadt wagons participating in the Tucson Rodeo Parade each year, keeps the name of Ronstadt alive.

The Ronstadt House was designed by architect Henry Trost and is on the National Register of Historic Places.

4th Avenue

West University Historic District includes two commercial areas, one on 4th Avenue and the other on University Boulevard.

(10) This sketch is from the corner of 4th Avenue and 5th Street. It shows the trolley car line that runs along 4th Avenue, to the 4th Avenue underpass. This car line connected the University of Arizona and its surrounding residential area to downtown Tucson. 4th Avenue is the location of the very popular street fairs held each year.

Coronado Hotel

(11)

This is one of the few examples of the frenzy of building done during the 1928-29 period when hotel development was given priority to accommodate tourist business then flourishing and encouraged by railroad promotion. 550 new rooms were added in Tucson. Unfortunately, few examples are left.

This hotel was built in 1928. It served the community until 1974 when it was closed. It remained closed until 1990 as it did not meet the new building codes.

The Downtown Development Corporation took over and plans were developed to use the property for subsidized low-income housing for the elderly and handicapped. By March 1991 the restoration was complete. They kept the original wood ceilings, stairways, and floors. The transoms were restored to the original look.

Introduction to Armory Park Historic District

In 1974 Armory Park was declared a city historic district covering approximately 30 city blocks. This area was largely settled after 1880 with the coming of the Southern Pacific Railway.

The railway brought new building products for home construction, mainly lumber. This changed the style of construction from adobe bricks to eastern-style frame or stucco homes which the newcomers to the territory felt more comfortable with.

Today Armory Park looks very much like it did at the turn of the century with its Victorian Queen Anne, mission, and Spanish colonial revival styles.

Map No. 3 Armory Park Historic District

Map Site No.

1. Blenman House (private residence)
2. Willard Hotel
3. Carnegie Library
4. Mormon Memorial
5. World War II Memorial
6. Spanish American War Memorial
7. Military Plaza
8. Safford School
9. Roskruge House (private residence)
10. Kitt House (private residence)
11. Schneider-Healy House (private residence)
12. Temple of Music and Art
13. Glenwood Hotel
14. Velasco House
15. St. Joseph's Academy
16. Temple Emanu-El

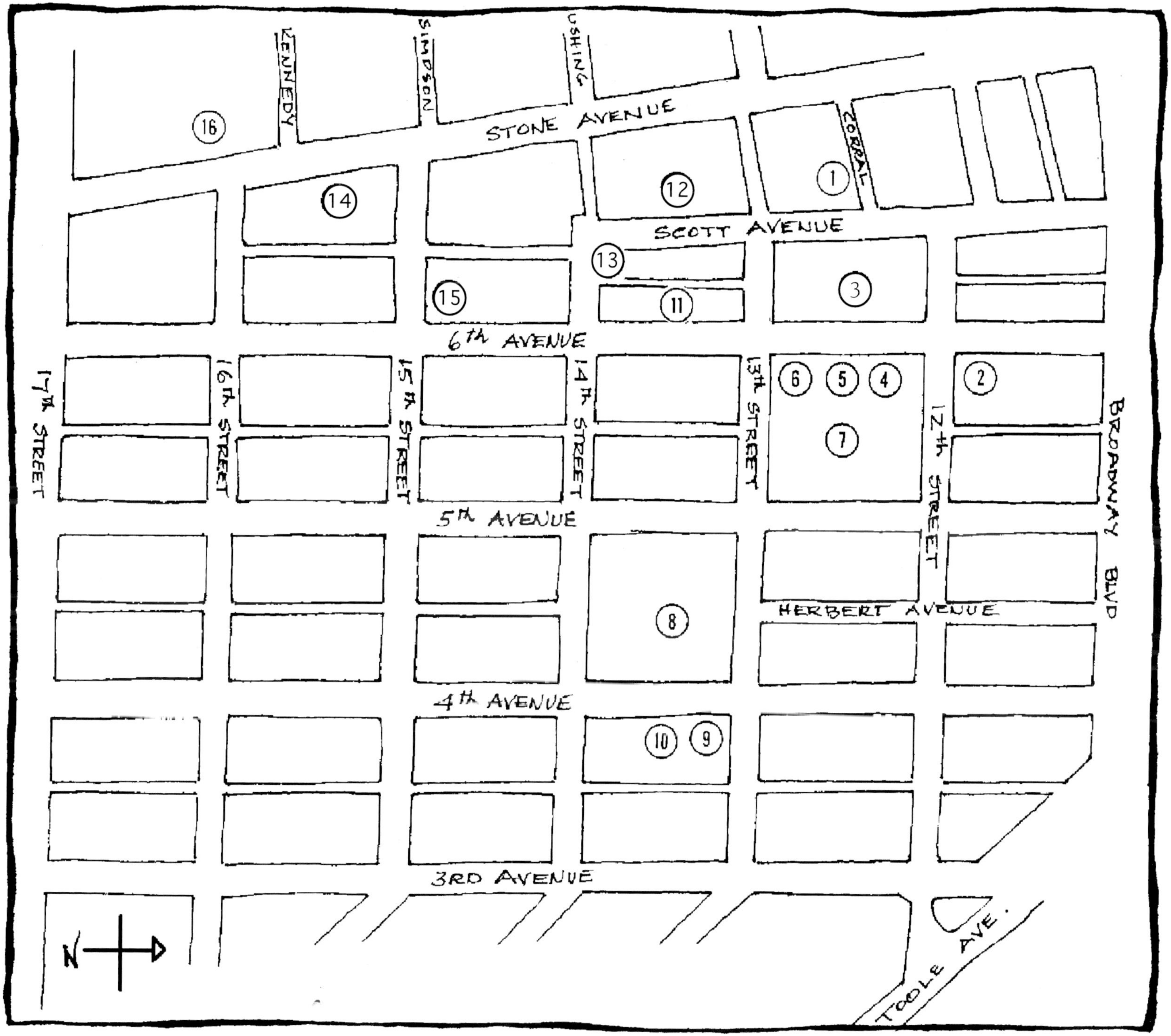

Map No. 3 Armory ParK

The Blenman House

Built in 1878 – with 22"-24" Adobe Walls

private residence

1 "Judge" Charles Blenman was born in 1860, in Devonshire, England. He became a solicitor in Temple Court, London. In 1891 he left England for San Francisco, then on to Tucson, Arizona, arriving here on the 24th of May, Queen Victoria's birthday.

Charles Blenman came from an Old English seafaring and naval family and his two sons became outstanding U.S. Naval officers. Charles Jr. became a navy pilot and, in 1942, a newspaper report credits Captain Blenman for shooting down 18 enemy planes in the Pacific War Theater. William became an Admiral.

The "Judge" practiced law from this home for many years. The purely honorary term "judge" was bestowed on him by his friends and colleagues who enjoyed his wit and hospitality.

He was remembered for the flagpole he had erected at his home. He would raise the flag at sunrise and lower it at sunset on national holidays. He was one of the charter members of the Tucson Elk's Club. The Blenman Elementary School is named after the "judge".

The Willard Hotel 1902

2

First called Hotel Casey (the owner), the name was changed immediately when Willard Wright and Charles Fleming signed a seven year lease with Casey for $250 a month. One year later Wright tried to renegotiate the terms of the lease because they were not making ends meet.
They rented rooms ---

American Plan - $2.00 per day and up   European Plan - $1.00 per day and up.

Casey, apparently turned the water off forcing guests, including the then territorial governor Brodie, to find other lodgings.

William Siewart, a professional chef, took over proprietorship. He was noted for making candied flowers using violets, roses, and other flowers via solar cooking, surely one of the first solar cooks in the country.

The hotel faces a park that has been known as the Military Plaza, Washington Park, and now as Armory Park.

It remained the Willard Hotel until 1944 when it was remodeled into the Pueblo Hotel and Apartments. A pool was added as well as the sign that had the swimmer animated with neon lighting tubes, a first for Tucson.

In 1984 the hotel was condemned by the city of Tucson and was occupied by transients and a large number of cats.

In 1991 it was rescued by six Tucson businessmen who purchased the hotel and have restored it beautifully.

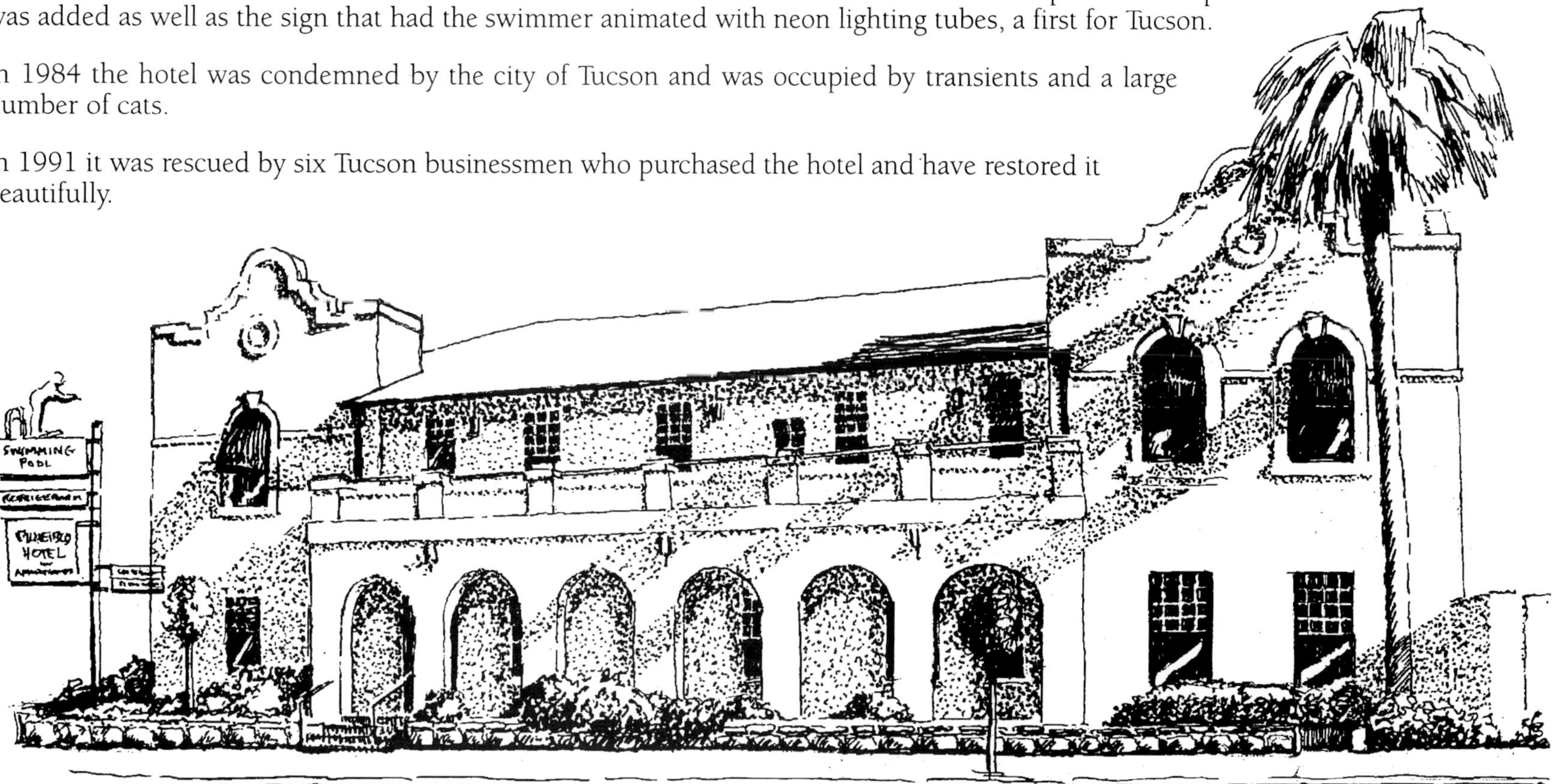

Carnegie Library

(3) The Carnegie Library opened in 1901. The architect was Henry Trost who designed the classic temple front with decorative mouldings and statuary.

In 1941 the ornate copper rotunda collapsed during a fire and was never replaced. Twenty years later, a semicircle addition covered the beautiful front entrance of the building. The addition has since been removed. Two additional wings were added and much of the library's decorative pieces were removed. In addition, a large wall, with metal gates, was built in 1961 to "keep winos from loafing around the front door."

By 1990 the library closed and moved to its new location at Alameda Street and Stone Avenue. The Children's Museum moved in during 1991.

Merrill Pingree Freeman

In 1920 the will of Tucson banker, Merrill P. Freeman, also a regent and chancellor of the University of Arizona, bequeathed $11,000 for an elaborate and circular bench of marble at the entrance to the library.

The back of the bench depicts a man and woman, symbolizing day and night, and two young children offering a gift to the dawning day. Brass letters in the marble platform read:

"To the memory of those pioneers of Arizona who have given their lives that we might live in peace and unafraid in this sunkissed borderland."

A 1940 photograph depicts the man and woman sans clothing, but in later years it appears they had been modestly clothed. The bench was designed by Bernard Maybeck and the sculpture work was done by 22-year-old Beniamino Bufano of San Francisco. In 1975 the bench was restored by the Armory Park Neighborhood Association for $5,000, which were the proceeds from a historic home tour.

CUMING

4

The Mormon Memorial

The Mormon Battalion, under the command of Colonel Cooke, was one of the three military units sent from the east to capture California from Mexico. 500 Mormon men enlisted but never trained as soldiers, in Iowa, in July 1846. They marched southwest and arrived in Santa Fe, New Mexico, in October along with about 40 wives and 50 children. By the time they were ready to leave Santa Fe, the women and children along with some of the men were too ill (even a leader, Captain James Allen had died of malaria), so they were sent to Salt Lake City. The 390 remaining men continued their march.

When the Mormons neared where the town of Saint David is today they had permission to shoot some wild cattle for meat. Furious bulls attacked the men and the engagement became known as the "Battle of Bulls". This was the only battle they fought on the way to California.

As the tired battalion neared Tucson Presidio, which still housed a Mexican garrison, the Mormons had the choice of a detour of 100 miles around Tucson or going straight through the Mexican fort. They choose the latter course and the Mexican authorities withdrew their troops. The Americans remained for about three days. The battalion raised the first American flag over Tucson on December 16, 1846, eight years prior to Tucson becoming a U.S. Territory in 1854. They inserted a flagpole into the mouth of a cannon on El Presidio's southwest bastion, approximately where Father Kino's Memorial stands today. The Battalion arrived in San Diego in January 1847, after a six month march of over 2000 miles.

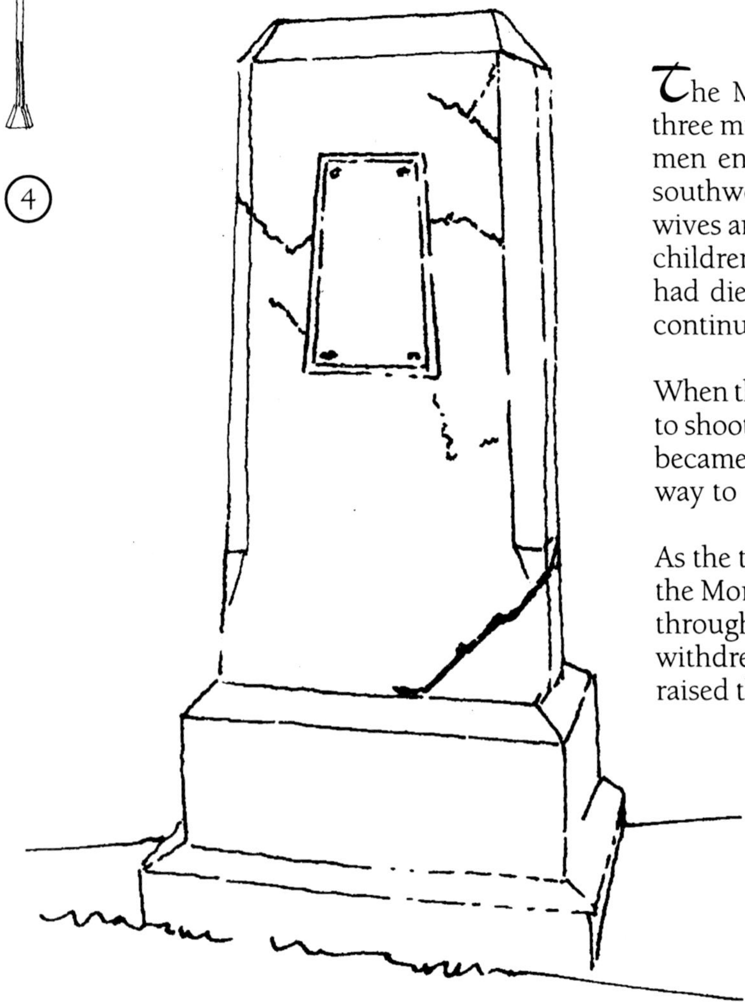

Erection Supervised by
M-men and Gleaner Girls
of the
Central Arizona District
of the
Church of Jesus Christ
of Latter-Day Saints
June 13, 1937.

To the Mormon Battalion

Which under command of Col. Cooke, in the course of their 2000 mile infantry march to the Pacific Coast, arrived and raised the first American Flag in Tucson. December 16, 1846.

The Military Plaza

Tucson, at the time of the Civil War, was a city divided, with most of its citizens sympathetic to the southern cause.

The Union soldiers were ordered to Fort Fillmore, N.M., to defend New Mexico and Arizona from the Confederate Army. The only civil war battle fought in Arizona was at Picacho Peak in April, 1862. Three Union men were killed and three captured. Additional troops arrived from California and the Confederates fled Tucson for New Mexico, along with most of the Anglo-American citizens of Tucson.

(7)

These Union troops took possession of Tucson in May, 1862, and by June there were 11 companies of infantry, 2 cavalry, and 2 artillery batteries camped at this location. The path from this military camp to El Presidio was called Camp Street, later changed to Broadway Boulevard.

This site was used until September, 1864 when it was abandoned. However, at the conclusion of the Civil War in 1865, the Plaza was re-activated as Fort Lowell, for troop service against the Apaches. In 1873, the camp was moved to the new Fort Lowell site.

(5)

Spanish-American War Memorial

(6)

There were 392,000 men and women who served in the 1898-1902 Spanish American War. Nathan Cook, the last surviving veteran, died in Phoenix on September 10, 1992 at the age of 106.

In Memory Of Those Who Served

Spanish American War 1898-1902

Cuba Puerto Rico Phillippines China

Lest You Forget

1917 WORLD WAR 1918
DEDICATED TO THOSE
WHO SERVED

LEST WE FORGET

8

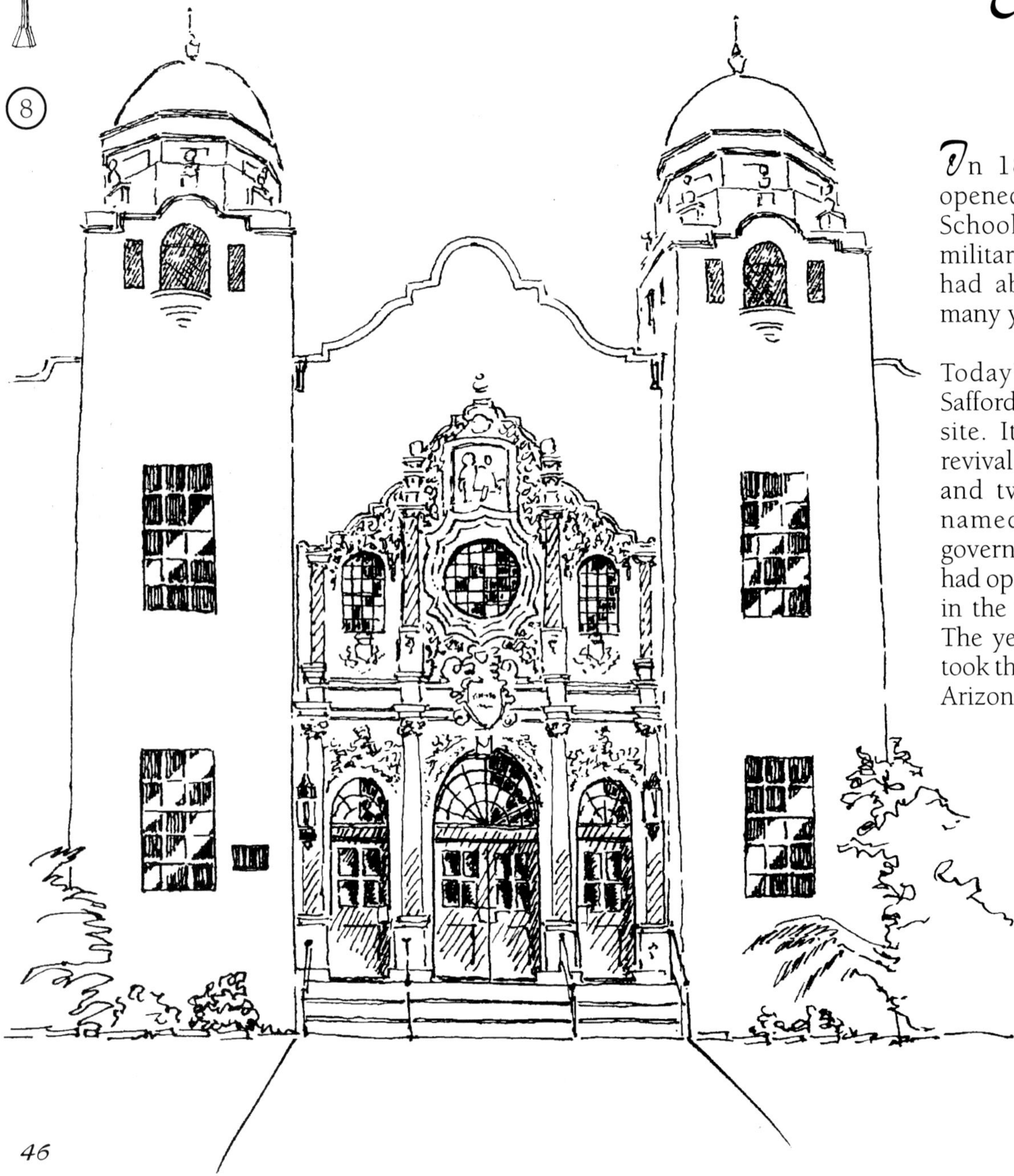

The Safford School

In 1891 another new school opened in Tucson called Safford School. It was built next to the military plaza which the military had abandoned for Fort Lowell many years before.

Today's building is the second Safford Middle School built on this site. It was built in the mission revival style with its elaborate entry and twin towers. The school is named after Arizona's third governor, Anson P. K. Safford, who had opened the territorial legislature in the then capitol city of Tucson. The year was 1870. The governor took the lead in public education for Arizona's children.

The Roskruge House

private residence

9

In 1872 George Roskruge, born in Cornwall, England, and sixteen other men left Denver on foot for Santa Fe. They moved on to Arizona and arrived in Prescott two months later.

Roskruge found work with the deputy U.S. surveyor and very shortly was transferred to Tucson as a draftsman for the surveyor general. In 1875, Roskruge was asked to draw up plans for the new public school on Congress Street. He named Kitt Peak after his sister, Mrs. Phillipa Kitt. He eventually became surveyor general and a University of Arizona regent.

Roskruge built this Queen Anne style home in 1896 which was designed by the same architect who designed "Old Main" on the U of A campus.

George Roskruge is given credit for designing numbered streets to run east/west and numbered avenues to run north/south after his survey of 1893. S.W. Foreman had surveyed and mapped the townsite in 1872 and Major Fergusson before that in 1862.

The Kitt House

private residence

10

This home was built in 1899 by William & Katherine Kitt on land given to them as a wedding present by George Roskruge. Kitt Peak is named after William Kitt's mother, Mrs. Phillipa Kitt, who was George Roskruge's sister.

Katherine Kitt came to Tucson from California and taught at the Safford School, although she is best remembered for starting the art department at the U of A.

The Schneider-Healy House

private residence

(11)

Joost Van Hemert Schneider and his wife, Rosemary, came to Tucson from California in 1902. Joost was in the land and cattle business. He served as a member of the Tucson City Council. Joost built this home in 1902, (Henry Trost, architect), when the only other building around was the convent up the street (St. Joseph's Academy).

Gustav Van H. Schneider, their son, was born in 1885 in Cornwall, California, and lived in Tucson 50 years. He worked as a civil engineer for the Southern Pacific Railway Company. He never married. Gustav became an authority on Old Tucson and as such served as a consultant and technical director for Columbia Pictures during the filming of "Arizona." The story was about Tucson during the period of 1870 to 1888. He was also responsible for editing 'The Original Tucson Diary of George Hand' written from 1875 to 1887.

Elizabeth Healy was Gustav's sister and was educated at St. Joseph's Academy. She married Thomas Healy who was working for the U.S. Government in Cuba where he died of malaria in 1930. Elizabeth then moved back into the family home with her brother Gustav. She was manager of the Temple of Music and Art. She was active, as secretary, in the Saturday Morning Music Club and had been a member since 1919.

The Temple of Music and Art

The Temple of Music and Art is the culmination of Madeline Dreyfus Heineman's dream. Mattie was born in Nevada City, California, of German-French parents. About 1900 she married Simon Heineman and moved to Tucson.

(12) Mattie Heineman, in 1906, started a Saturday morning music club with twelve women and was instrumental in bringing many great names in the music world to perform in frontier Tucson. Simon died in 1924. Many of the friends of music and art she had developed, in a quarter of a century, came to her aid. Her dream of an artistic center for the city of Tucson neared fulfillment when the groundbreaking ceremony took place on November 11, 1926.

The Temple of Music and Art included an auditorium seating 1000 people, a display room for paintings, a stage large enough for a full symphony orchestra, a small recital hall, dressing rooms, studios, etc., and a tearoom. The final price amounted to $180,000. Alexander Berger gave $100,000 as well as financing the WWI Memorial at "Old Main" U of A.

This cultural center was built through the efforts of the Saturday Morning Music Club. The grand opening October 28, 1927, starred violinist Jascha Heifetz. Many world renowned artists followed upon the stage and in the galleries while local talent also gave recitals and concerts.

Original home of the Tucson Fine Arts Association and the Tucson Boys Chorus. Restoration was begun in 1976. Listed in the National Register of Historic Places.

The Glenwood Hotel

13

The hotel was originally built in 1908 with 32 rooms. Dr. & Mrs. W. Purcell purchased the hotel. Dr. Purcell was killed in an auto accident in 1910 and the hotel was sold again.

The hotel stood vacant for two years and in 1986 the building was owned by the Armory Park Investment Group who converted the rooms into permanent resident apartments.

Again in 1993 the hotel was converted - this time into an office center.

The Glenwood Hotel is listed on the Register of National Historic Places.

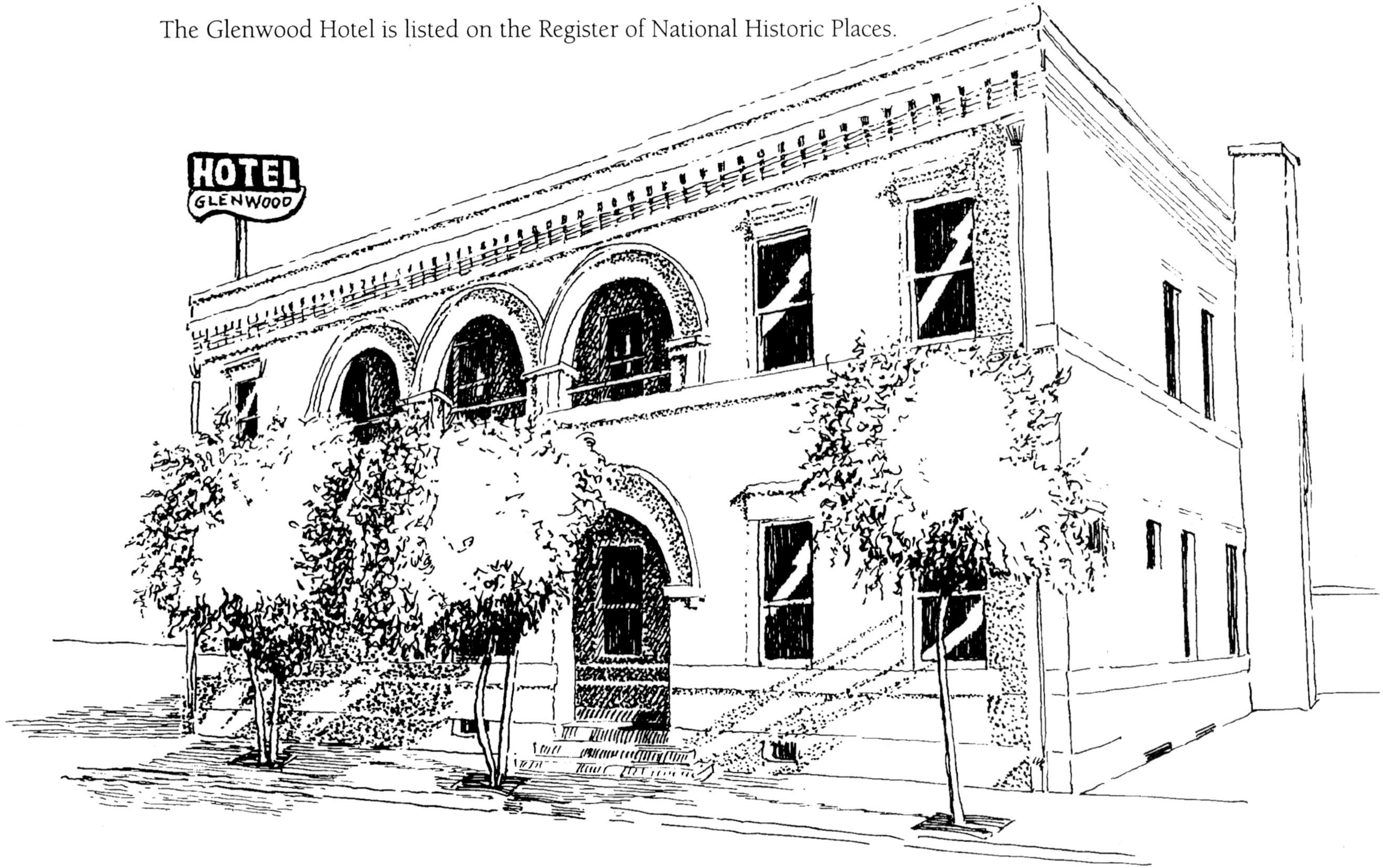

Carlos Y. Velasco House

This 1850s house had the hip roof added in the 1880s. Velasco was born in Hermosillo, Mexico, and arrived in Tucson sometime in 1860. He sold his general store in 1878 to publish Arizona's first Spanish newspaper which he set up in the southernmost room of this home.

14

The *El Fronterizo* started in 1878 and was printed on a Washington hand press originally brought from the East to Tubac in 1859. Velasco purchased this press from the *Arizona Citizen*.

The first *Weekly Arizona* newspaper was printed in Tubac March 3, 1859, on this same Washington hand press. The press had been shipped to St. Louis by rail from Cincinnati and by freight wagon to Tubac. The *Weekly Arizona* was moved to Tucson from Tubac in 1870 and renamed the *Arizona Citizen*.

The old press was returned to Tubac and is on display in the Tubac Historical Museum.

This house, dating from the 1870s, was purchased by Carlos and Beatriz Velasco in 1878. The same year, Velasco began publishing the newspaper *El Fronterizo*, which continued until his death in 1914. This building was the office and print shop. The house at the rear was the Velasco residence. Prominent in civic affairs, Velasco was a principal founder of Alianza Hispano Americana, a national fraternal insurance society. A National Register site.

St. Joseph's Academy

15

The seven Sisters of St. Joseph of Carondelet arrived in Tucson in May, 1870. They lived in a convent and school adjoining the Old St. Agustin Cathedral. A few foundation stones remain of the church in a park on Church Avenue between Congress Street and Broadway Boulevard.

Eleven days after the Sisters' arrival, they opened the first school in Tucson. The original convent school quarters contained only three rooms and by the early 1880s the number of students had outgrown the accommodations.

A new site was located at the northwest corner of 15th Street and 6th Avenue and the new St. Joseph's Academy opened as a school for girls in 1886.

The new building, constructed of stone vs the old adobe building, was one story high. Over the next ten years a second story was added as you see it today.

In the early 1930s, St. Joseph's moved to a Wilmot Road location and the old Tucson property could not be sold for $100,000, and later became Immaculate Heart Academy.

St. Joseph's Academy on Wilmot Road had a devastating fire in 1948 but was rebuilt. In 1969 St. Joseph's Academy closed forever.

However, this massive building,[much of the stone work was done by Jules Flin (El Charro)], stands as a memorial to those original seven Sisters of St. Joseph of Carondelet.

16

Temple Emanu-El

Jewish pioneers, among Arizona's earliest settlers, began arriving in the 1850s and for half a century they worshipped in private homes and rented quarters. In 1904 the Hebrew Ladies Aid Society, now the Sisterhood of Temple Emanu-El, was established formally to provide social services and religious needs. One of the goals was realized when Temple Emanu-El, the territory's first synagogue building, was erected at a cost of $4712. It opened on the eve of the Jewish new year "Rosh Hashanah," October 3, 1910. The congregation worshipped here until 1949.

This plaque is the only one provided in three languages: English, Spanish, and Hebrew.

In 1996 the Stone Avenue Temple Project celebrated the return of the deed on the Old Synagogue to Jews and Gentiles alike who want to save the 2500 sq. ft. building.

Across the street is the Mexican Consulate, in a restored turn-of-the-century home.
(Estados Unidos Mexicanos Agencia Consular)

Introduction to West of the Santa Cruz

Seven years before Don Hugo O'Conor founded the present site of Tucson on August 20th, 1775, there was another Tucson.

Just a short distance west of the Santa Cruz River under the base of Sentinel Peak ("A" Mountain) was the site of an Indian village. Father Francisco Garces was in charge of the mission at San Xavier Del Bac at this time. He visited the village, in 1768, and called the settlement of Indians "Tucson" which means, Schuk-Shon in Indian language, "base of black mountain".

He established a mission at the village and by 1773 a lookout tower, a wall, a chapel, and a granary had been built.

As we now know a "convento" was built between 1797-1810 and then abandoned by 1828 as the new Tucson, east of the Santa Cruz River, had become the hub of activity.

Map No. 4 West of the Santa Cruz

Map site No.

1. Garden of Gethsemane and Felix Lucero Park

1a. Tucson's largest tree

2. Sentinal Peak

3. Convento Site

4. Warner's Mill

5. Mortuary Chapel

6. Mission San Xavier Del Bac

7. Grotto of Lourdes

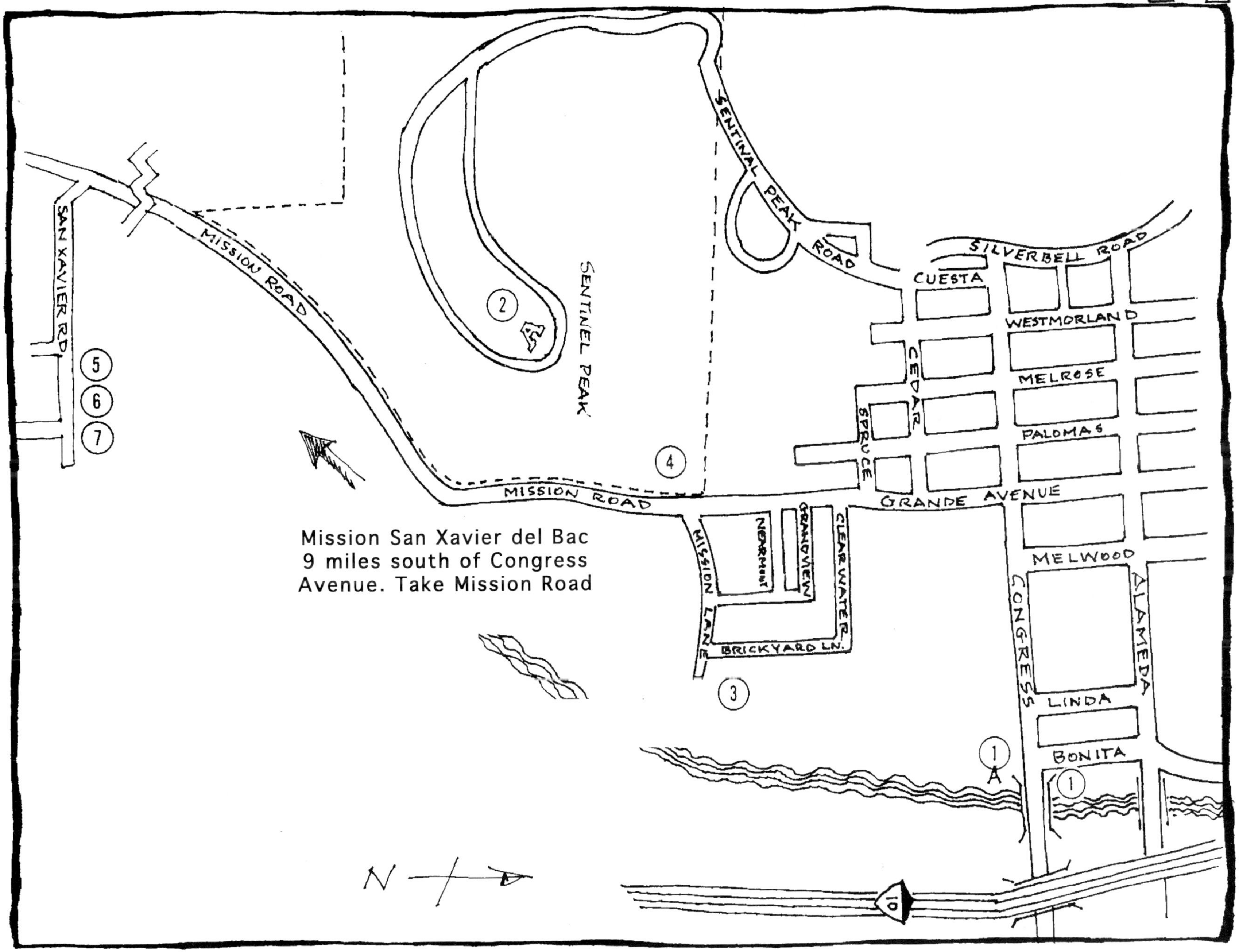

No. 4 West of the Santa Cruz

A

1

Garden of Gethsemane Felix Lucero Park

The Knights of Columbus in Cooperation with Tucson Parks and Recreation
assist in the care and maintenance of Garden of Gethsemane Statuary and Park.
This community project was commenced February 1981
to preserve the Art of Felix Lucero.

Donated by Charles Edward Francis

Felix Lucero 1895 - 1951

The artist sculptor was born in Trinidad, Colorado. In World War I, he lay critically injured on a forgotten battlefield. He vowed to God and to himself if he survived he would dedicate the remainder of his life to the sculpturing of religious statues for which he had a natural talent. After 20 years of this pious work in various parts of the country he arrived in Tucson in 1938. Heartbreak and pain walked with the artist during his sacred efforts.

The sculptures include the Last Supper, Jesus on the Cross, Joseph and Mary, a Reproduction of the Tomb, and a theatre-like castle with an open front displaying a scene of Pontius Pilate washing his hands and another of a Legion of Roman soldiers. The statues are all made of concrete, sand, and debris recovered from the Santa Cruz River.

The work, started in 1945, continues to survive the ravages of time, floods, and many acts of vandalism. The Garden of Gethsemane was first moved in 1971 for the construction of the Congress Street bridge. The current facility was constructed in 1982 as part of the Santa Cruz River flood control improvements.

The present facility represents a cooperative effort between the City of Tucson, the State of Arizona and the Downtown Development Corporation.

ONLY

A

(1) A

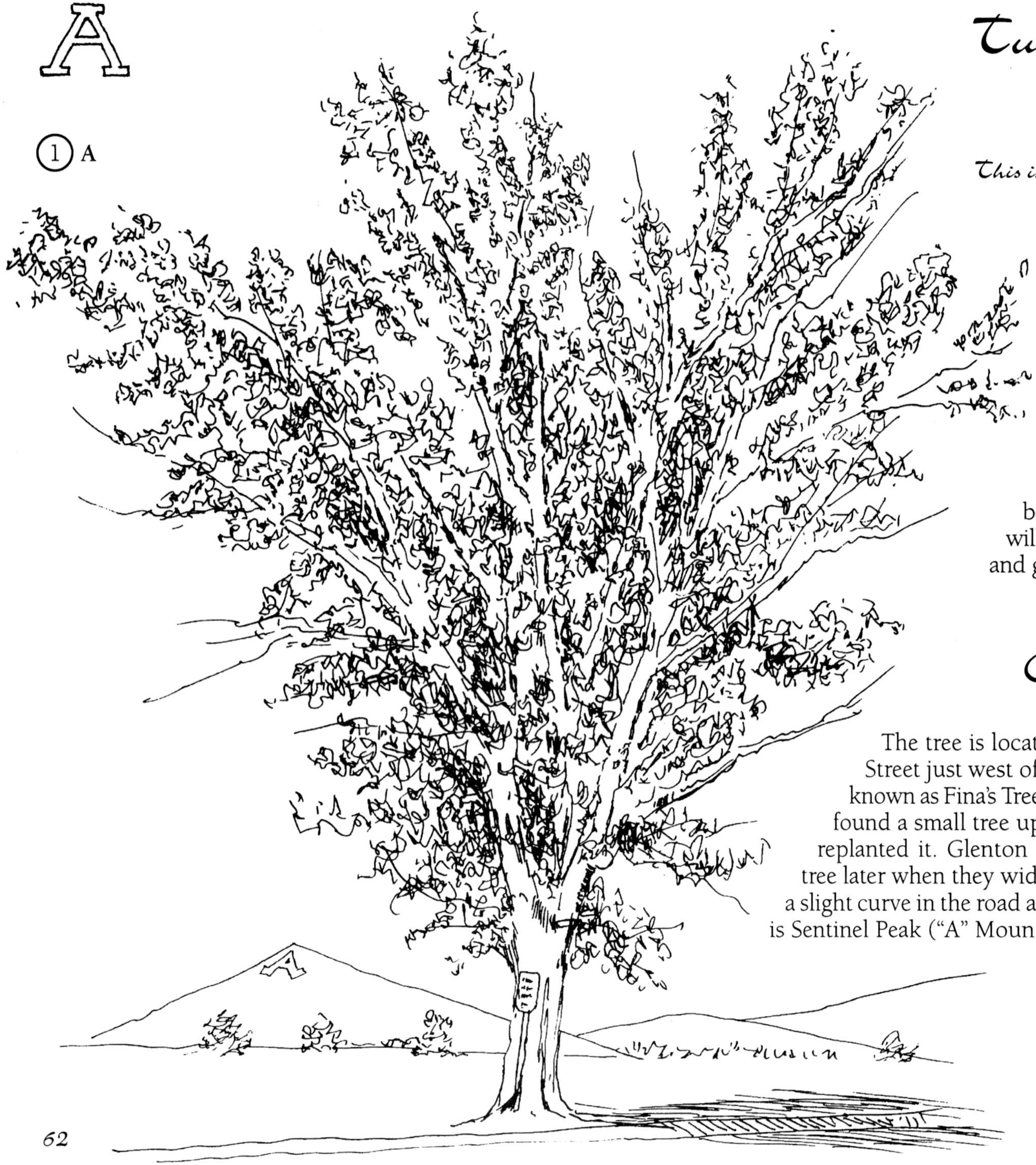

Tucson's Largest Tree

This is a fine example of Eucalyptus Rostrada

It measures 13 feet in circumference, has a diameter (dbh) of four feet, it is growing in a very favorable location a region of deep rich soil and its roots are undoubtedly down to permanent ground water.

It is young and vigorous and it will be of great interest to see how large it will get. Let us guard it and protect it and give it a chance.

City of Tucson

The tree is located on the south side of Congress Street just west of the Santa Cruz River. It has been known as Fina's Tree. A young girl named Defina Bravo found a small tree uprooted after a storm in 1910 and replanted it. Glenton Sykes, a city engineer, saved the tree later when they widened Congress Street and there is a slight curve in the road around the tree. In the background is Sentinel Peak ("A" Mountain).

Sentinel Peak

A

②

Below this 2900 foot peak the Santa Cruz Valley was farmed by the Hohokam Indians as early as 800 A.D. When Spaniards arrived in the 17th century the Hohokam had vanished and settlements of Pima people had dotted the valley. One called "Schuk-Shon", meaning "at the foot of the black mountain," was pronounced "Tucson" by the Spaniards. The hill was the lookout for these early Indian and Spanish settlers who lived in fear of hostile raiders. The whitewashed stone "A" was constructed by University of Arizona students in 1915.

Sentinel Peak
used as a lookout and for signal fires
by the Indians prior to and since 1692
and later by early settlers

DAUGHTERS OF THE AMERICAN REVOLUTION

DAR Marker
1938

The Convento Site

Father Francisco Garces, in 1768, who was in charge of the Mission San Xavier Del Bac, called the Pima settlement at the base of Sentinel Peak ("A" Mountain), Tucson. There is no record of buildings existing there other than the "pit houses" of the Indians.

In 1771 a wall and lookout tower were completed. By 1773 a small chapel, along with a granary, had been erected.

The most impressive building was the "convento," a two-story adobe about ninety feet long and forty feet wide. It had 5 rooms upstairs, 2 downstairs, and a wide arched hall running through the center. This building was probably built on the site of the earlier 1773 chapel.

It is believed the "convento" was built between 1797-1810 by Father Juan Llorenz, who completed the San Xavier Mission Church in 1797.

By 1828, the "convento" was abandoned. A report of the building's condition was made by Joaquin Quiroga in 1843 that the "convento" had lost its windows and doors and the roof had fallen in. Early in the 1900s the building was still standing. In 1899, a University of Arizona publication said: "the people of Arizona have every reason to thank the antiquarian association for their efforts to preserve the interesting ruins and relics of prehistoric civilizations. There is one instance, however, that we wish to call attention to. Just across the Santa Cruz River, a mile from Tucson, are the remains of the San Augustine Mission, the first manual training school founded in the U.S. and remarkable for its interesting history and antiquity." Nothing was done. The mission lies beneath Tucson's city dump.

There is a strong opinion that the site of this "convento" and surrounding village area of the Pima Indians should be considered as the founding of Tucson, in 1770, when the wall with lookout towers was built by Captain Anza. However, the 1775 date and location of the El Presidio wall built by Captain Allande is considered the historical founding of Tucson.

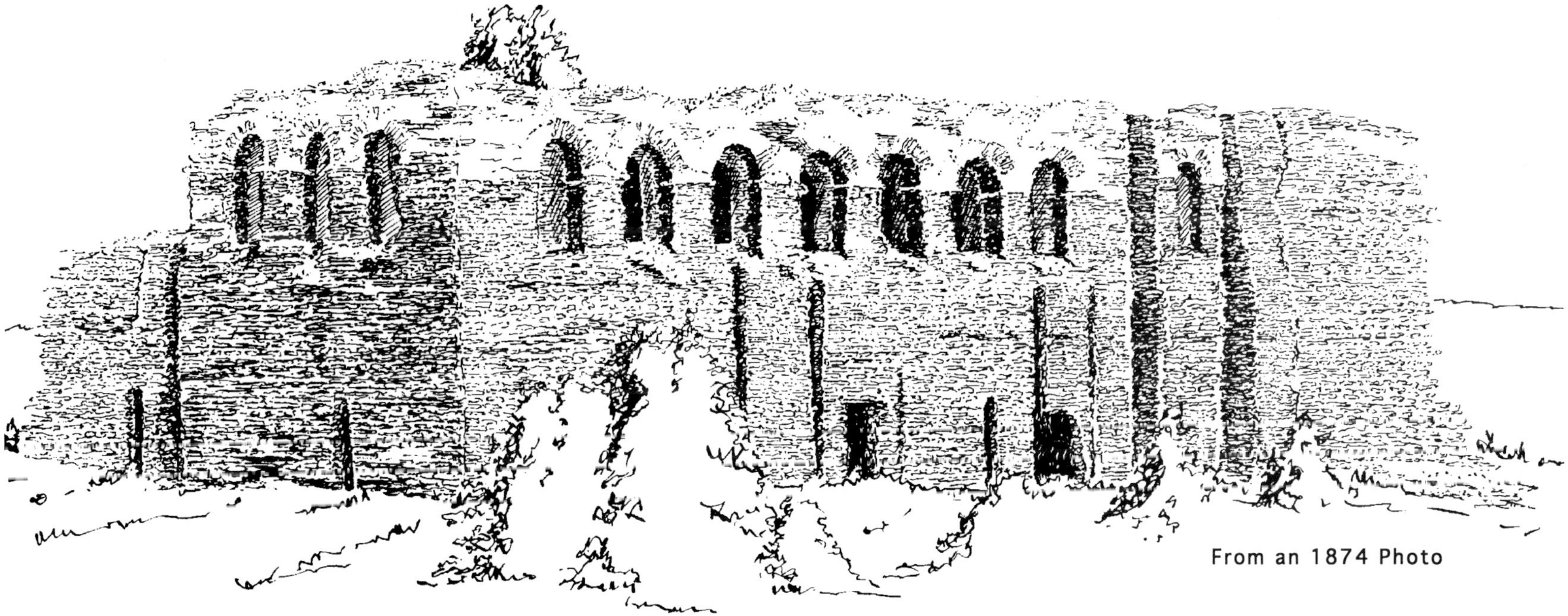

From an 1874 Photo

A

Warner's Mill

(4)

Solomon Warner, a pioneer merchant who came to Tucson in 1856, constructed a two-story flour mill here in 1875. To the south he built a dam across the Santa Cruz River creating a small lake. From there a flume ran along the base of the mountain feeding a raceway and waterwheel which turned two sets of heavy millstones capable of grinding about 100 bushels of locally grown wheat a day. A small stamp mill, powered by the same waterwheel, was used to crush ore from Warner's mines.

Solomon Warner was born in 1811 in New York State. He lived in Tucson from 1856 to 1899. As a proprietor of a general store near the Presidio gate (Alameda Street and Main Avenue), he ran freight wagons from Yuma to Tucson.

Warner was a "union sympathizer" and when he heard the Confederate Army was on its way to Tucson in 1862, he fled to Sonora, Mexico where he started ranching and married a rich Mexican widow. He left Mexico in 1870 and was severely wounded by Apaches on his way back to Tucson.

In 1874-75 he built the water mill, and converted it to steam in 1878. However it was not competitive with the Eagle Steam Flour Mill so it was sold.

Unfortunately, Solomon suffered for many years from his wounds and died in poverty in 1899.

Mortuary Chapel

This chapel was used as a resting place for the deceased until the requiem service was held in San Xavier Church.

There is a marble marker on the floor where two priests were interred after their removal from the old mission at Tumacacori in 1935.

The Latin Inscription reads:

"Here rest from their labors two renowned missionaries who departed this life in the midst of an arduous and very successful career in this region

Reverend Father Baltazar Carrillo, O.F.M.

October 9, 1795

Reverend Father Narciso Gutierrez, O.F.M.

December 21, 1821

Their bodies, transferred from the Old Franciscan Mission at Tumacacori, Arizona were interred in this mission of

San Francisco Xavier

February 21, 1935"

The old cemetery has the fourteen stations of the cross inserted in relief in the surrounding walls.

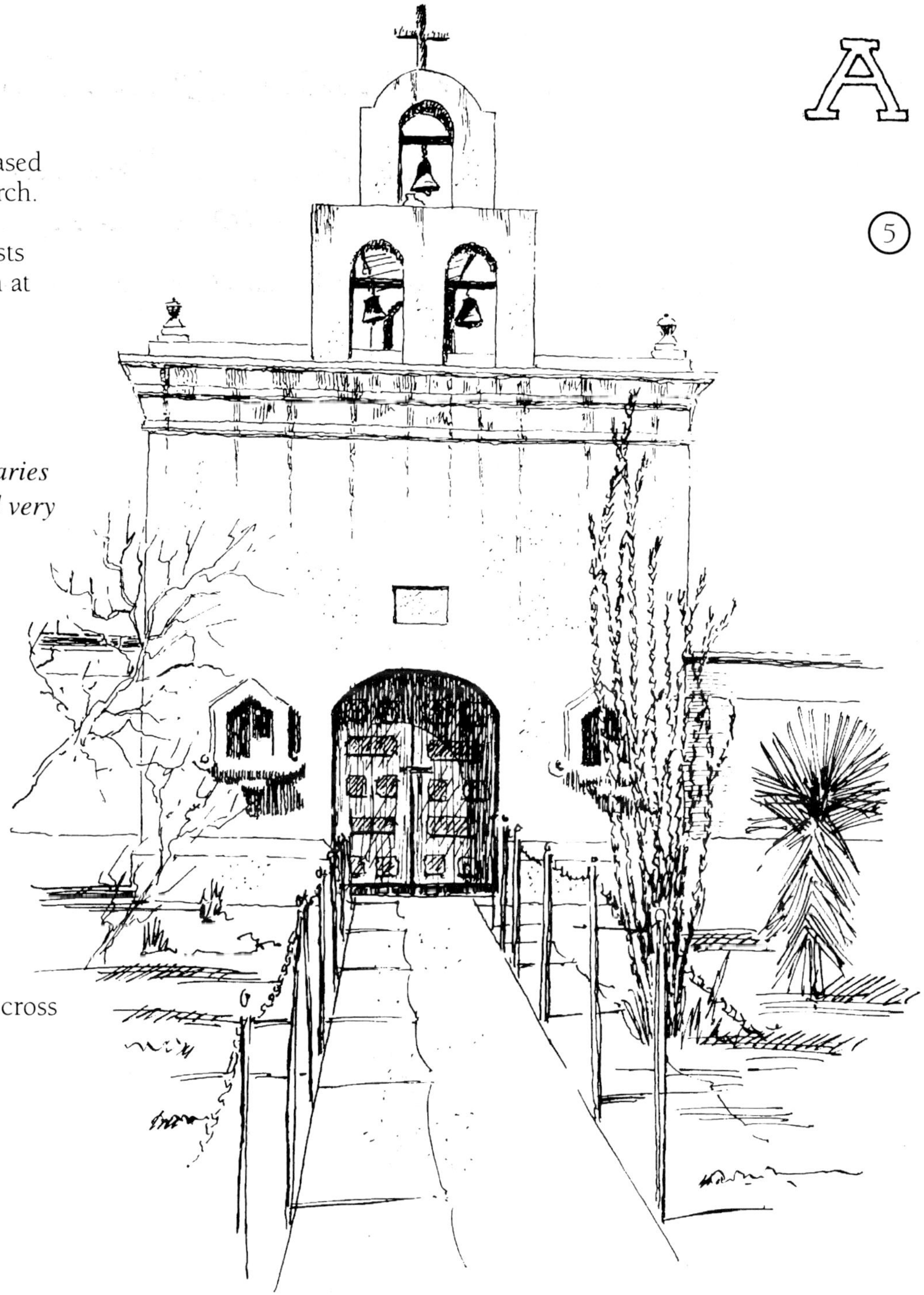

A

5

A

Mission San Xavier Del Bac

La Paloma Blanca Del Desierto —

White Dove of the Desert

⑥

The mission church is situated in the Santa Cruz Valley 9 miles south of Tucson on Indian lands. Bac means "a place where water appears."

Father Kino, a Jesuit missionary, first visited Bac in 1692. In 1700, he laid foundations for the first church about 2 miles north of the present site. After the Jesuits were expelled by Spain, in 1767, the Franciscans took over. In 1768, Father Garces established his headquarters here. His successors, Father Bautista Velderain and Juan Bautista Llorenz, tackled the fourteen year job of hit-and-miss labor to build this mission church during the 1783-1797 period.

Today there are still questions of who the architect was, why the east tower was never completed, and who were the skilled workmen and artists.

This building is rated as one of the finest examples of mission architecture in the United States. This mission has been in continuous use since it was built. Look for the cat and mouse at the entrance, for they say "when the cat catches the mouse the world will end."

The Mouse and The Cat

A

A

7

Grotto of Lourdes

Erected by the Bishop of Tucson AD 1908
the fiftieth anniversary of the Wondrovs
appartions of the Blessed Virgin Mother of God
at the Grotto of Lovrdes

On the eastside of the San Xavier Mission is a cross mounted on a cone-shaped hill. Many years ago this was an active volcano. After the coming of the missionaries the priests erected this cross as a place for the Indians to pray that the volcano would not become active again.

Later, in 1908, Bishop H. Granjon, of the Tucson Diocese, constructed a permanent shrine commemorating the world famous Shrine of Loudres in France. This encouraged the Indians to continue using the site for their own devotional needs.

The Grotto appears to be fully completed but the construction of an entrance, patio, and gardens has been left unfinished.

This small brass plaque is found below and to one side of the statue of the Virgin Mary.

Donated by friends and relatives in memory of Raul S. Martinez

Introduction to Miscellaneous Sites

Not all of the following nine buildings or sites are on the National Register of Historic Places but all are interesting to visit.

These sites are within the metropolitan Tucson area and it would be necessary to visit them via public transportation or automobile.

The maps on each page will give you an indication of the building's location and all are easily accessible.

Index for Miscellaneous Section

St. Philip's in the Hills Episcopal Church

(1)

St. Philip's in the Hills Church is one of the most beautiful in Southern Arizona. It was styled after Spanish colonial missions with its 36" side walls, massive Mexican cedar doors, with 18th century hardware, cloistered patios, and the gardens with an 18th century stone cross from Mexico.

During the day the interior of the church is bathed in light from the dramatic and large arched clear glass window behind the main altar. This window offers an ever-changing view of the Catalina Mountains which are to the north of the church.

The original church was dedicated on Christmas Eve, 1936, as a chapel in the Catalina Foothills, by the Rev. George Ferguson, its first rector. The chapel was built by developer John Murphey and designed by architect Josias Joesler.

In the beginning the church could only seat 198 persons but after expansions in 1957 and 1986 the nave of the church now seats 450 plus 125 in the chapel. Additional seating was added to the east and west transepts.

Visiting the church and walking through the patios and gardens takes you back in time and to many countries. The church received, as gifts, 14th and 15th century paintings, a Spanish baroque altar in the baptistry, 17th century marble reliefs, Mexican stained-glass windows, chapel cross from the 14th century, a crucifix carved by an American Indian dating to about 1750, and basswood figures of the Virgin and St. John circa 11th or 12th century. The altar frontal was woven in London, England, and the candlesticks are Spanish.

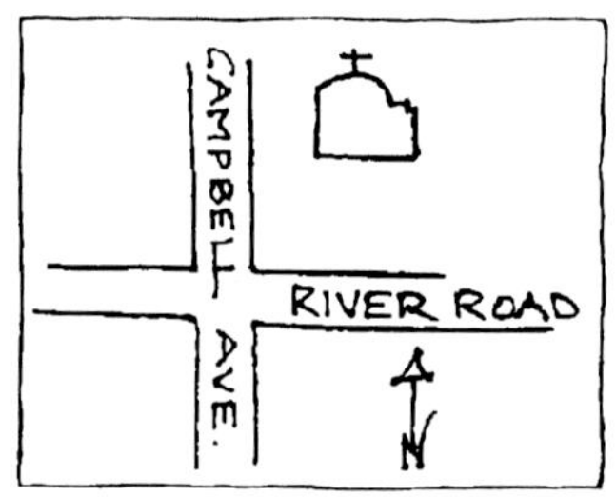

1. St. Philip's in the Hills

The Arizona Inn

2

From 1900 to 1930 Tucson's population grew from 7500 to 32,500. In 1909 Tucson's first rate downtown hotel opened as the Santa Rita with 180 rooms. In 1929, the second major downtown hotel opened as the Pioneer Hotel with 250 rooms.

Prior to the turn of the century there were smaller hotels called the Palace, Occidental, and Cosmopolitan. Even the Roman Catholic Cathedral and Convent of San Agustin had been converted into a hotel.

By 1928, the El Conquistador had opened on Broadway Boulevard on the site of the present El Con Mall. About the same time Mrs. Isabella Greenway, a widow who had experience in building several homes with her mining engineer husband, contemplated building a resort to house furniture manufactured by disabled World War I veterans. Mr. and Mrs. Greenway had been involved in politics and veterans affairs for many years. In 1927, Mrs. Greenway founded "The Arizona Hut" with the original headquarters in the old Trinity Chapel building tucked into the corner of the Scottish Rite Cathedral. Furniture was made in a manufacturing plant on Congress Street where 40 veterans were employed. However, sales did not keep up with production. In 1930, with a warehouse full of furniture, Mrs. Greenway took out a building permit for the Arizona Inn. Her plan was to use the excess furniture in the Inn.

She was convinced that Tucson needed a western and desert style hotel away from the downtown area. Cottages were built that allowed the guests to live in a hotel and have the privacy they would have in their own homes, thus the concept was started of a group of homes surrounding a garden. The Arizona Inn was born and has served visitors for almost 70 years as a "homelike cottage hotel."

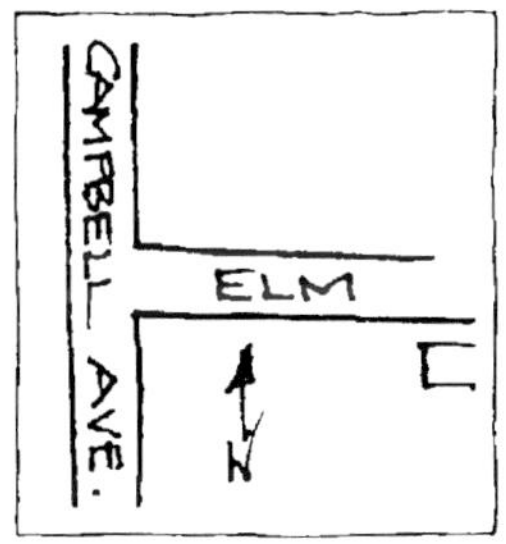

2. Arizona Inn

El Conquistador Hotel in Three Parts

Water Tower:

3 Originally built by developer John W. Murphey, as a plain, steel-legged, 50,000 gallon water tower to serve the new communities of Colonia Solana and El Encanto as well as the new El Conquistador Hotel. The hotel was built in 1928. The neighbors complained so much about the ugly tower, a stucco facade was added in 1932.

It is thought that Roy Place, a Tucson architect, was responsible for the design. Roy Place also designed the old Pima County Courthouse which was built in 1929.

In 1944 the City of Tucson bought the Murphey's Water Company and used the tower until 1967. In 1968 the El Conquistador Hotel was demolished for a shopping center (El Con Mall). By 1975 the city prepared to tear down the water tower. Activists took over and were able to get the tower listed in the National Register of Historic Places in 1980.

In 1991, the City of Tucson designated the tower as a city landmark. $100,000 was spent on its restoration with money donated by the city and the Arizona Heritage Fund. The tower was rededicated in 1994.

The Portal:

The portal or entryway to the El Conquistador Hotel is now the guard gate at the Sin Vacas ("without cows") Estates at the corner of Ina Road and Camino Sin Vacas.

The Dome:

The copper dome from top of the hotel is now on a building in a small shopping complex at the northeast corner of Rudasill Road and Oracle Road.

3. El Conquistador Hotel in Three Parts
(Water Tower)

1890 Locomotive at Himmel Park

Plaque 1994

(4)

The Southern Pacific Railway arrived in Tucson on March 20, 1880. For the first time the community had a reliable access to the rest of the country. This access changed Tucson in many ways from architectural styles to furniture and clothing. Tucson had become a real part of the United States.

Locomotive #1673, a Mogul 2-6-0 type engine, was built by Schenectady Locomotive works in 1900 and logged over 1,000,000 miles for the Southern Pacific Railroad Company, primarily in Southern Arizona. In 1955 it was donated to the City of Tucson to mark the 75th anniversary of the arrival of the railroad to the community. Since 1992 it has been listed on the National Register of Historic Places.

This historic locomotive has been on display at Himmel Park since 1962, having been moved from the front of the Arizona Historical Society Museum. It was originally powered by coal and was converted to oil in 1905. The engine and coal tender is over 36 feet long and weighs 75 tons. It was in use for over 50 years. This was the engine that appeared in the filming of the movie *Oklahoma* in 1954.

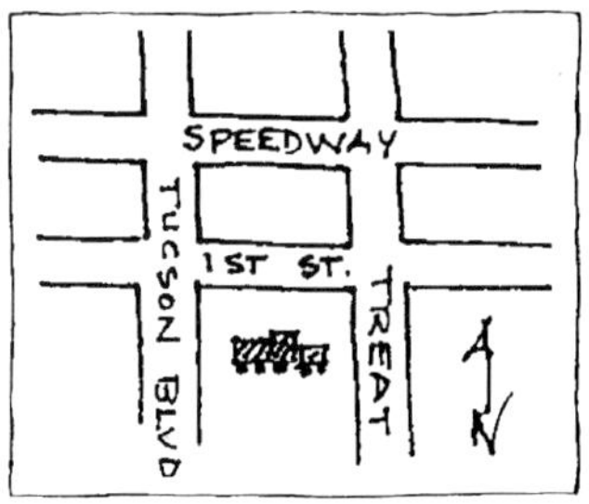

4. Himmel Park

Presented to the people of Tucson
March 20, 1955 by Southern Pacific Company
commemorating the 75th anniversary
of the arrival of the first train in the Pueblo of Tucson

Father Kino Statue

1987 was the 300th anniversary of Father Kino's arrival in Arizona. A committee was formed to raise funds to erect a memorial to this event. This statue now stands at the corner of East 15th Street and South Kino Blvd.

There is an earlier memorial to Father Kino in El Presidio Park near the intersection of Alameda Street and Main Avenue. In 1936 it was presented to the City of Tucson as a gift by the Kino Memorial Association.

The casting of Father Kino on his horse is 15 ft. high and was designed by Mexican sculptor Julian Martinez, who donated his work. There are two more identical statues, one in Magdalena, Sonora, Mexico, where Father Kino died and was buried. Another is in Trento, Italy, where he was born.

Julian Martinez also designed the General Francisco Villa Statue in the 20th of August Park at Broadway Blvd. and Church Ave.

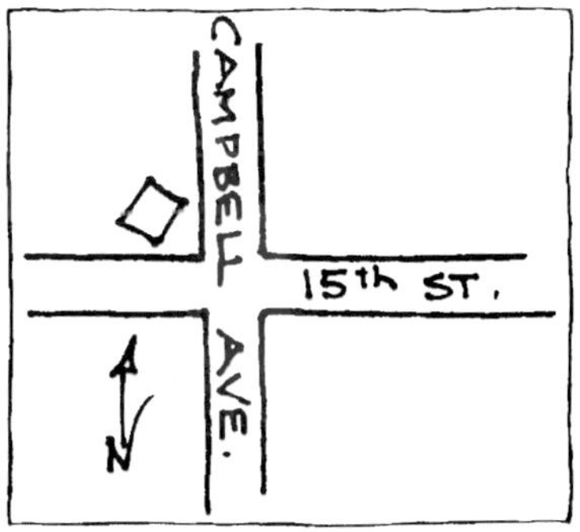

5. Father Kino Statue

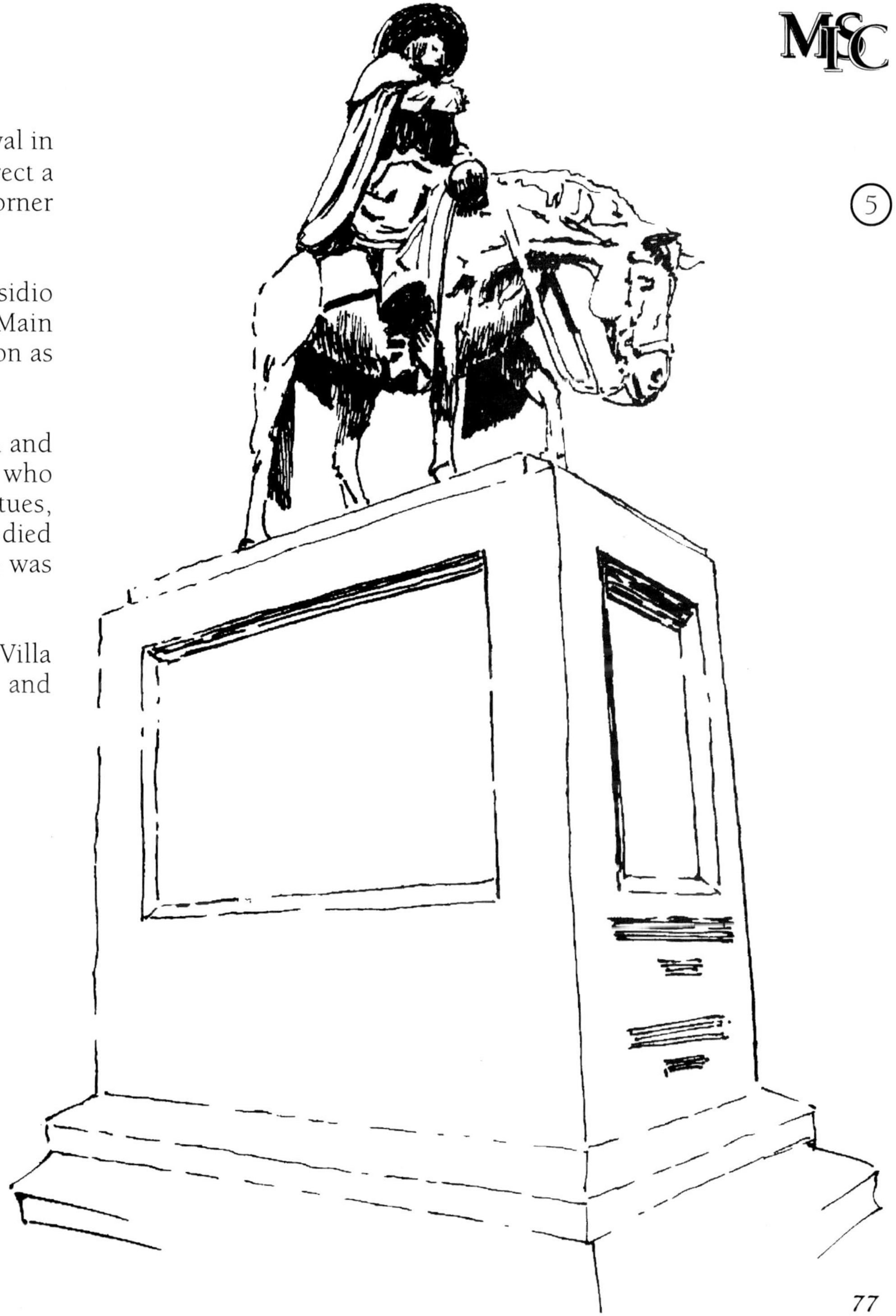

MFSC

5

Holy Family Church

(6)

corner stone

Holy Family Church
erected by
The Bishop of Tucson
A.D. 1913
Manuel G. Flores, Builder

Statue of Christ to the West

Tucson a Christo Rey
Los Hijos a Su Madre En El IV Centenario De Su
Aparicion Tucson AZ

Statue of St. Therese to the East

A Teresa C De Pacheco -In Memoriam-
Su Hija Amelia Pacheco

In 1922 Holy Family School opened but only lasted two years because mines in the area closed. Later on Nuns of the Discalced Carmelite Order, who fled from Durango, Mexico, during the persecution of the Catholic Church in Mexico, used the facility. Later it became the Dunbar School (segregated) and finally the John Spring Elementary School.

In 1926 the rectory was built and in 1928 the parish hall was completed. In 1929 the first monument in honor of Christ The King was erected - a first for Arizona as well - about the same time the Statue of St. Therese was erected in the gardens.

Carmelite Fathers from Holy Family Church also served the congregation of the Village of El Fuerte at the Chapel of San Pedro - Fort Lowell until 1948.

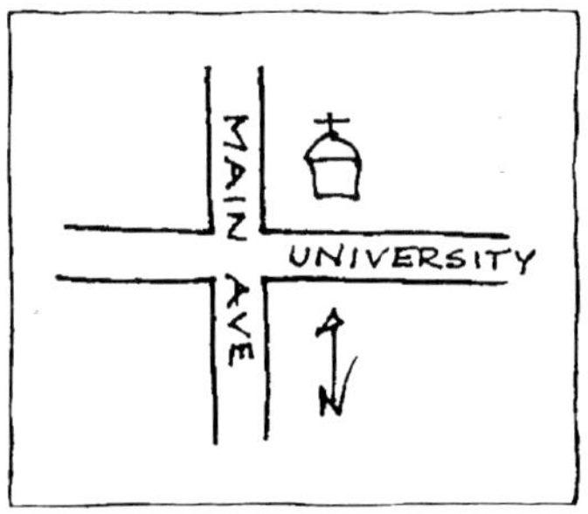

6. Holy Family Church

Santa Cruz Church

Holy Cross

(7)

This church was built in 1916 using the same builder, Manuel Flores, as the Holy Family Church and was dedicated in 1919. The candelabra, solid oak pews, statuary, chairs, and baptismal font, donated by the first parishioners for the opening, are still in use. The window frames and baseboards are made from cherry wood.

The church was made of adobe bricks, made on the Tohono O'Odham Reservation, by Indians from San Xavier Mission. The Indians were paid $10.00 for each 2000 bricks. Bishop Henry Granjon, the second Roman Catholic Bishop of the Diocese of Tucson, directed the construction based on his drawings, which relied on his earlier architectural studies.

The courtyard was patterned on church courtyards in Spain and the complete church is an architectural look-alike of a Spanish convent in Avila.

On November 11, 1918 - Armistice Day - the Bishop climbed up the 90-foot tower steps to ring the church bells announcing the good news of peace.

The "Academia De La Santa Cruz" opened in 1920. In 1922 a well was dug and a windmill erected to irrigate an orchard promised by the Bishop. Tragedy struck, in 1924, when a dynamite bomb blew the doors down, smashed all the windows, and later caused a large part of the roof to give way.

The church is now on the National Register of Historic Places.

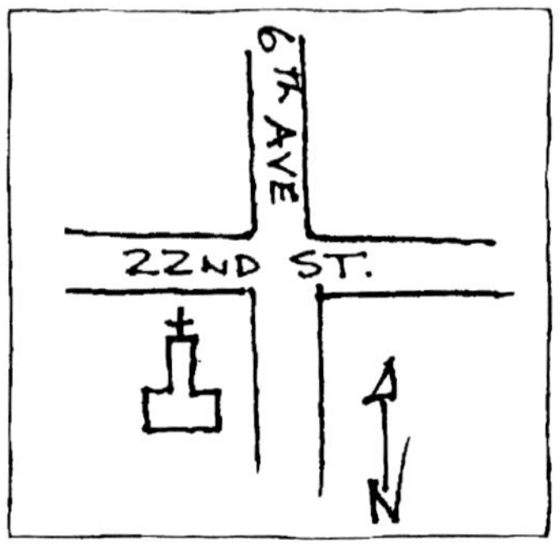

7. Santa Cruz Church

Veterans Hospital

Veterans of World War I living in Tucson, in the early 1920s, existed in shacks helped only by the Red Cross.

8 There was a facility called the Pastime Dance Hall which could house 40/50 sick veterans, far fewer than was needed. Thousands of men, who had suffered from gas exposure during the war, had come to Tucson for their health.

By 1928 the government had built this veterans hospital. An addition was added between 1929-1930 with outside labor brought in for major construction projects in and around Tucson, i.e., the Consolidated Bank Building, the Pioneer Hotel, and the Post Office. Once the projects were completed the men were out of work and had to go on "relief". It was the start of the Great Depression in 1930.

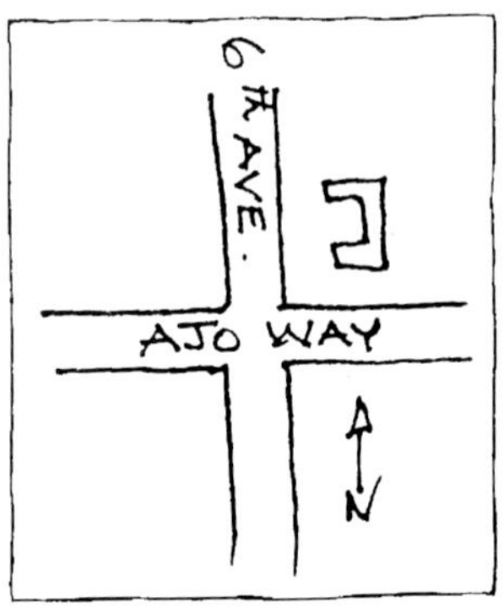

8. Veteran's Hospital

Thanks

First Municipal Airport

(9)

Lindy Beacon

Lindy Beacon was dedicated at the Municipal Airport by Charles Lindberg in September, 1927, when he visited the city with his ***Spirit of St. Louis*** after his transatlantic flight. A contribution of the Beacon was made to the City and was presented by Mayor White. Later the Beacon was moved to Ryan Field. The original site of the Municipal Airfield is where the rodeo grounds are today. An original tin hangar is still on the site and contains many Ronstadt antique wagons and others used in the annual rodeo parade.

Arizona Historic Site

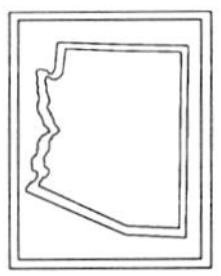

This ground was the location of the First Municipal Airport in the United States.

The Tucson City Council approved the financing for the airport July 21, 1919
and the City of Tucson in cooperation with the Tucson Chamber of Commerce
Established and constructed the Airport
The first plane landed Nov. 20, 1919
Swede Myerhofer, Pilot.

Upon receipt of an official letter from Brig. Gen. "Billy" Mitchell of the U.S. Air Service urging the City of Tucson to provide a Municipal Airport, Mayor O.C. Parker and Allen B. Jaynes, President of the Chamber of Commerce, appointed a joint committee consisting of the following members:

City of Tucson	Chamber of Commerce
O.C. Parker	Allen B. Jaynes
R.E. Fishburn	Orville S. McPherson
H.S. Corbett	Monte Mansfield
Stanley Kitt	Kirk Moore
Folsom Moore	E.J. Anderson

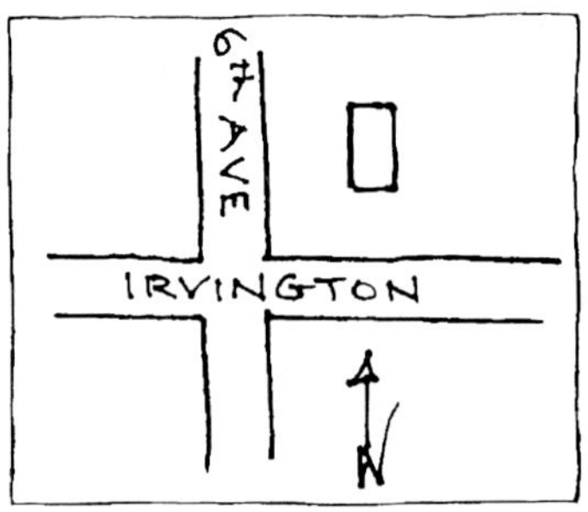

9. First Municipal Airport

The committee purchased the 84-acre site from L.H. Manning for $30.00 an acre. A $5,000 loan from the Consolidated National Bank paid for the property and all necessary improvements and airport facilities.

B
TUCSON RC
MAIN ENTRANCE

Introduction to Tubac and Tumacacori Mission

Tubac

plaque located at the entrance of the town

Tubac is the oldest continually occupied European settlement in Arizona. It was first mentioned by name in 1726 when Father Campos, a Jesuit missionary, baptized some Indian children here. A presidio was established after the Pima uprising of 1751 and in 1775 Captain De Anza led an expedition from Tubac to found San Francisco. The center of mining activity in the 1850s Tubac had a school in 1885 and Arizona's first state park in 1959. Tubac now has a community of artists.

Tubac Map

A 1776 map of Tubac was prepared by cartographer Joseph De Urrutia for Inspector Marques De Rubi. The original is in the British Museum obtained by the English when they captured a Spanish ship returning to Spain from the New World. A copy is on display in the Presidio Museum and is the main source of determining which sites and buildings are recorded in this book.

When the Pima Indians revolted in 1751, San Xavier and Guevavi were plundered. As a result a presidio was established at Tubac. This fort, manned by 50 soldiers, became the center of the first recorded white settlement in Arizona. Late in 1775 the Tubac Garrison was moved to Tucson. Later Tubac was regarrisoned by Pima Indian soldiers until the fort was abandoned in 1848. The population of the town moved to Tucson.

Map No. 5 Tubac & Tumacacori Mission

Map Site No.

1. Churches in Tubac
2. School House
3. Pennington House
4. Herreras House
5. Lowe House (private residence)
6. Territorial House
7. East House
8. Otero House (private residence)
9. Brownwell House (private residence)
10. Espinoza House
11. Tubac Presidio
11a. Printing Press
12. Otero Hall
13. Rojas House
14. Presidio Park (Baca Float #3)
15. Sabori House (private residence)
16. Old Garrett Stable (private residence)
17. Garrett House (private residence)
18. Cementery
19. Otero Ranch
20. San Cayentano Del Tumacacori
21. The Campo Santo

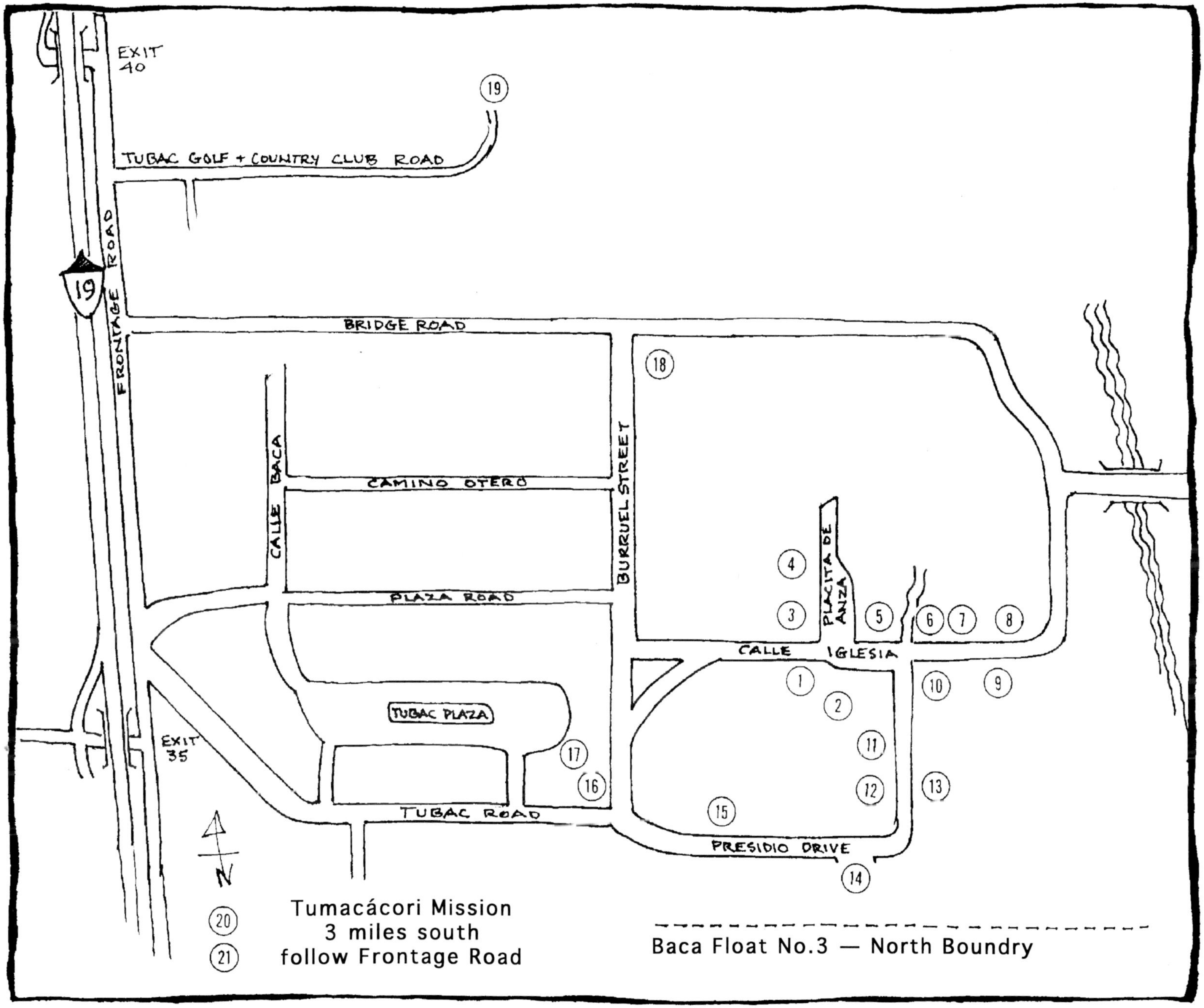

Map No. 5 Tubac and Tumacacori Mission

Churches in Tubac

1

Several Tubac churches have stood on this site. The first, a shelter built by Jesuit missionaries in the early 1700's, was administered from Tumacacori. About 1760 Captain De Anza built a chapel for presidio soldiers. A later church was visited by Father Machebeuf, Vicor General from Santa Fe. Father Duval of Nogales built a church in 1910, which crumbled in the heavy rains of 1914 and was rebuilt in 1920.

Santa Gertrudis De Tubac was the first name of this church. The Spanish map of 1766, by Urrutia for Inspector Marquis De Rubi, shows a church building on this site. In 1796, there is a report that a Franciscan Padre was in residence and an adobe church was complete. The crucifix over the altar came from a church in Yucatan, Mexico, and dates to about 1750.

Tubac was often deserted by its residents because of continuous Apache raids. By 1848, the church roof had gone with only the walls standing and by 1858 the church was beyond repair. A drawing, by J. Ross Brown (1858), shows the church with three bell openings. From about 1858 to 1885, Francisco Solano Leon donated a two-room house to be used as a church but Tubac was deserted much of the time during that period.

Services were held in the schoolhouse built in 1885. By 1900 the church was beyond repair; it was used as a pigsty. Father Duval (buried in Sacred Heart Church - Nogales) constructed a new church in 1910. Very heavy rains fell in 1914-15 damaging the church and by 1920 the walls had fallen due to faulty construction.

A new church was built on the original foundation with the walls being stuccoed in 1929. Anna Maria Coenen and her daughter Anita Maria Maldondo along with Anna Burruel and Rosa Barragan Lim were the ladies responsible for raising the funds for construction of this latest church. The name St. Gertrudes was changed to St. Ann's in their honor.

The church was strengthened and restored again in 1974-75. During that period a 250-year-old shrine that served to give travelers a spiritual break was going to be demolished as it was in the way of the new Tucson-Nogales freeway. It was moved from its location beside the old Nogales highway to the rear of the church where it is believed the original church cemetery is located.

Old Tubac School House

15

T. Lillie Mercer and Sabino Otero built the first schoolhouse in 1885. Up to that time, classes were held at Otero's ranch and later in a schoolroom built at one end of the Otero store.

The one room dirt floored schoolhouse was also used for weddings, baptisms, and funerals until the church was rebuilt in 1910 by Father Duval. In 1907 the schoolhouse was enlarged with a hardwood floor installed and the roof replaced.

Sabino Otero was a very successful rancher and had a store in Tubac, which he sold to Mercer. The store contained a classroom and was used as Tubac's first school.

Mercer came from Boston in 1877 and was very active in Tubac affairs, including postmaster, after purchasing the Otero store. He also had mining interests and ran the Miner's Hotel in Tubac. He hired Sarah Black, the first school teacher, in 1884 for the new school. She taught in the Otero store until the school building was finished.

For unknown reasons, someone blew up Mercer's store and home in 1887. He and his family left Tubac to live in Nogales where he died in 1894. Mercer's daughter, Pauline Emma, born in January 1887, is said to have been the first white child born in Tubac.

Sarah Black, born 1834, came with her husband John from Maine. She taught in the new schoolhouse for three years from 1885-1888. She retired probably because of poor eyesight . Her husband John taught until 1899 when he was apparently dismissed for alcohol problems.

John and Sarah bought property from the widow of Henry Lowe in 1900. Unfortunately it was within the Baca Float #3. In 1918, Sarah, aged 84 and a widow (John died in 1911), was threatened with eviction from her Carmen home (now the Carmen Store). The deputies had her furniture, dishes, and all her belongings on the street before Sarah was able to make a deal with the Baca Float heirs. Sarah died in her Carmen home in 1929.

Tubac Schools

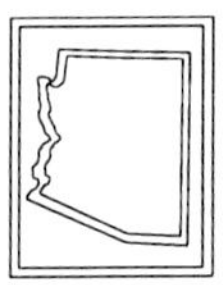

In 1789, Toribio Otero received the first land grant in this area in exchange for teaching school at his ranch. A school district was established in 1876 and in 1885 T. Lillie Mercer built this school, one of the earliest in Arizona. It was in use until 1965 and is now part of Tubac Presidio State Park.

Pennington House

3 This home was built in 1860. Elias Green Pennington was originally from South Carolina. He arrived in Arizona in 1857 as a widower with 12 children. He lived in the surrounding area during the years of 1860 to 1868 and was in Tubac in 1864. Finally he and his family settled in Tucson where he ran a sawmill near Church Avenue and Pennington Street.

Larcena Page was a married daughter of Elias and was captured by Apache Indians in 1860. She could not keep up with her Indian captors on their march back to their camp . They stripped her, cut her with their weapons, and threw her over a cliff thinking her dead. For fourteen days she crawled about the desert naked, hungry, and cold before being found.

Elias Pennington, his two sons, along with John, Larcena's husband, were killed by the Apaches.

Herreras House

The Pedro Herreras family was listed in the 1831 census. Pedro had left Tubac in 1860-1861 for Los Reales, a farming community near San Xavier Del Bac. In 1866 he moved back to Tubac to this house and served as postmaster.

The house was built in 1860, prior to the Civil War. The U.S. Army used the building as officers' quarters. Later, in the 1920s, the house was used as living quarters for the U.S. Border Patrol.

4

Lowe House

private residence

(5) Henry William Lowe was born in Germany, in 1849, as Heinrich Wilheim Von Lowenstein. He changed his name after his arrival in Arizona in 1867. He was in Tubac by 1882 and died in 1893. Henry and his wife, Marie, had 9 children. One, a son William, born in 1872, became an active Democrat. His home was a meeting place for politicians including Governor Hunt.

William Lowe had a large dairy farm and was the first, in the West, to use electric milking equipment. He operated the post office out of his home from 1905-1941. Every afternoon Romon Quintero picked up the mail at the railroad station across the Santa Cruz River and brought the mail, on his burro, to the Lowe home where it was sorted.

William Lowe died in 1946.

The house was built in 1904 and a major addition was added in 1914 to the west end.

Territorial and East House

The Territorial House was built in 1857, and was part of a row house including the one called the East House. These may have been built by Poston's Mining Company.

6

Charles Debrille Poston was born in Kentucky in 1825, and moved to San Francisco in 1851. He arrived in Tubac about 1854.

7

He saw the potential of Arizona mining and returned to Cincinnati, Ohio, to persuade investors to form the Sonora Mining Company in 1865. In 1859, William Wrightson came from Cincinnati as mine manager bringing with him a printing press. As soon as the press arrived it was used to publish Arizona's first newspaper ***The Weekly Arizonian*** in Tubac.

By 1882, Poston was not living in Tubac and had been criticized by J.A. Whitmore, the editor of the Arizona Citizen. They met, not by chance, and Poston took a pistol shot at Whitmore and luckily missed.

Poston prospected Arizona, formed the first mining company to invest capital, and developed mines in Arizona after the Gadsden Purchase in 1854.

He was elected the first delegate to Congress from Arizona in 1864. He was the registrar of the United States Land Office of Arizona from 1877 to 1880. In 1884 he was one of the founders of the Society of Arizona now called the Arizona Historical Society.

Sadly by 1899, the 20th legislature passed an act to appropriate $25.00 per month for Poston's subsistence. "Charles D. Poston is now over 70 years of age without income and feeble with age, and has but a few more years to live."

Poston died in a Phoenix shanty in poverty in 1902. In 1925 the DAR had his remains moved to a small butte north of town and erected a memorial marker.

Charles Debrille Poston

1825 - 1902

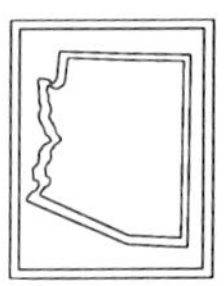

Poston, known as the Father of Arizona, came to Tubac in 1854 after Gadsden Purchase and established the headquarters of a mining company, with mines near Arivaca and in the Santa Rita Mountains. Mining activities were discontinued during the Civil War because of increased Apache Indian attacks. Poston was instrumental in promoting Arizona and helping it achieve territorial status separate from New Mexico in 1863.

This plaque is located at Burruel Road and Tubac Road.

6

East House

7

Territory House

The Otero House

private residence

(8) Ysidro Otero was Teofilo's son. He built and lived in this home in Tubac. Built ca. 1898 - 1913.

Near here Juan Bautista De Anza, Commandant of the Tubac Presidio, arrived from Sonora, Mexico, with a party of 177 persons and 140 mules. This was to be the final gathering place for an expedition to upper California to found a mission and presidio. The other purpose was to block the Russians from moving further south. The mission became known as San Francisco.

In late fall, 1775, the expedition of about 240 settlers and 40 soldiers left Tubac for the 1200 mile journey. They arrived at their destination in March, 1776.

The Brownwell House

private residence

A building appears on this site in Joseph De Urrutia's 1776 Spanish map of Tubac. The building, built prior to 1913, was greatly enlarged and renovated in the 1980s. It served as the home of Elizabeth R. Brownwell who was president of the Tubac Historical Society. She was responsible for establishing the Tubac Historic Library in 1976 and for placing the first plaques marking historic spots. (9)

Espinoza House

(10) A portion of this house appears to be standing on foundations of a building shown on the 1766 map. The southern building was built in 1861 with later additions in 1882. There were a number of Espinoza families in Tubac, Alcario 1864, Barsilio, Juan and Santos 1870, but it is believed that Inez Espinoza built this house.

Juan Bautista De Anza

1734-1788

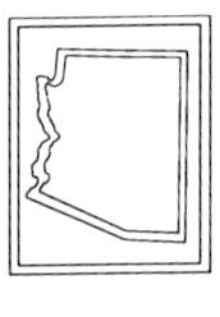

Captain Juan Bautista De Anza, son and grandson of presidential captains of New Spain, was commander of the Tubac Presidio from 1759 to 1775, the year in which he led an overland expedition to California to found San Francisco. In 1777 he became Governor of New Mexico. He is buried at the cathedral at Arispe, Sonora.

This plaque is located on Calle Iglesia and corner of Presidio Drive.

Tubac Presidio

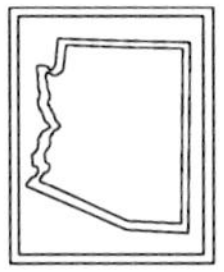

Here stood the original Spanish presidio or fort established as San Ignacio De Tubac after the Pima Indian uprising in 1751. Captain Juan Bautista De Anza was in command in 1775, when he led his famous expedition to California to found San Francisco. The Garrison was moved to Tucson in 1776, but Tubac was reoccupied by the Pima Indian soldiers in the later 1780s. In 1959 Arizona's first state park was established here.

11

The Printing Press

Here on March 3, 1859, the ***Weekly Arizonian*** was published, Arizona's first newspaper.

(11) A Edward E. Cross was the editor and was opposed to creating Arizona as a territory. Sylvester Mowry, a delegate to Congress, favored it and challenged Cross to a duel with rifles; fortunately both missed.

Mowry, Cross's opponent in the duel, bought the press and moved it to Tucson.

The Tubac Press was manufactured in Cincinnati, barged down the Mississippi to New Orleans, sailed around the Horn to Guaymas, then traveled by oxcart to Tubac. The ***Tucson Citizen***, ***Arizona Star,*** and the ***Tombstone Nugget***, as well as Arizona's first Spanish newspaper, ***El Fronterizo***, all have been printed on this press. It is back where it started and is on display and still operating in the Tubac Presidio Museum.

Presidio of Tubac

Garrisoned by Spanish in 1752
First town established in Arizona by Europeans here on March 3, 1859
The Weekly Arizonian was published ... Arizona's first newspaper
Historical Marker erected by Arizona Newspaper Association 1959

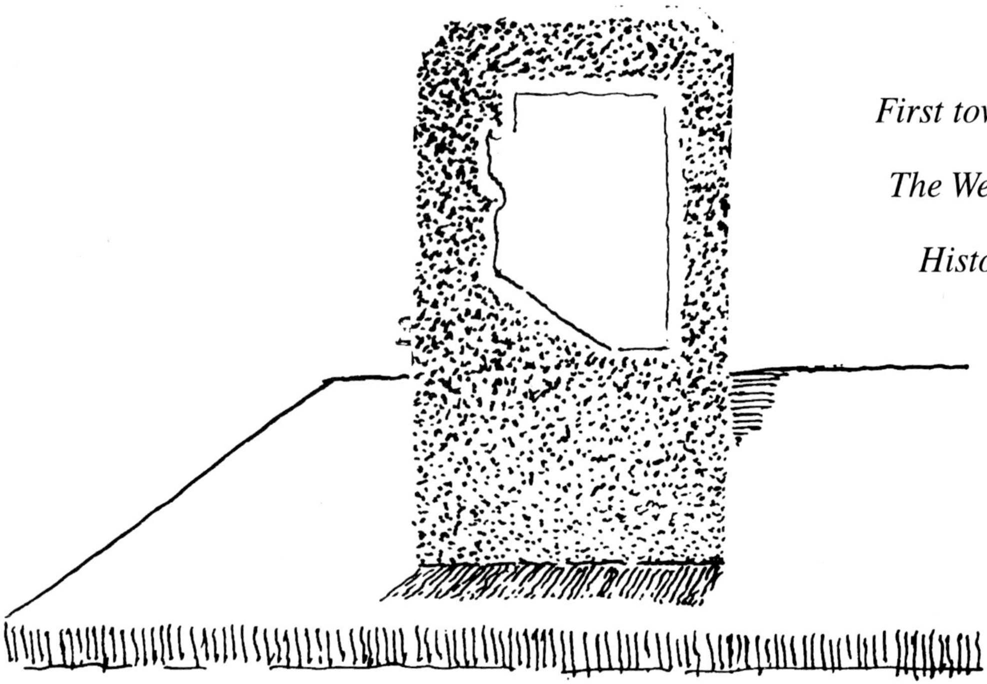

The marker is outside the front door of the State Park entrance.

Otero Hall

(12)

Don Toribio De Otero was given the first land grant in this area from the King of Spain. His great grandson, Teofilo Otero, had this hall built in 1914. Originally it was used as a community hall. As the Tubac schoolhouse became overcrowded the overflow students used the hall as a classroom. Urrutia's 1776 map shows a building in exactly the same location - the foundations appear to align up with each other.

Rojas House

(13)

Raimund Rojas (Reymundo Rojas) lived in this adobe house ca. 1882-1893. An addition was built on the south end in 1908. Luisa, his daughter, was born in 1893 in the building now in ruins behind the house. Luisa was the caretaker of the Tubac School for 21 years.

This building is on a lot originally owned by T. Lillie Mercer in 1882.

The ruins behind the Rojas building could have been an addition to Glassman's Hotel, 1876-1889, and first occupied by Mercer in 1877. Rojas was a victim of the Baca Float No. 3 debacle.

Two of his three lots were north of the boundary but the third fell within the Baca lands. Apparently, Raimund did not move his cattle off the third lot quickly enough so they were all shot dead by a deputy marshal.

Tubac Presidio State Historic Park Picnic Ground

14

On this site stood the commercial center of Tubac from the time of the Gadsden Purchase of 1854 to 1921. Ruins remain in this area of the original residences and stores. The fence, along the south side of the picnic area, is the northern boundary of the Baca Float # 3, land traded to Luiz Baca for land in New Mexico as a result of the Gadsden Purchase. All original Tubac buildings south of here were abandoned or torn down; only the foundations remain.

X marks the location if you are standing at the fence line. This was taken from a photo ca. 1918.

Baca Float Number 3

This was the northern boundary of Baca Float Number 3, one of five 100,000 acre grants made to the Baca family in exchange for land taken from them in New Mexico. An attempt was made to relocate this grant to include mines in the Santa Rita Mountains to the north, but in 1917 the grant was established here, and settlers on the land were evicted. Many moved north to present day Tubac.

Sabori House

private residence

There is very little information on this house. One fact we know, it is another of Tubac's homes that has been built over the foundations of a building found on Urrutia's 1776 map. There was a great deal of moving away from and back to Tubac over a period of years. It was abandoned in 1776 when the Garrison moved to Tucson, in 1850 saw the California Gold Rush, and in the 1860s there were epidemics of diseases and the Apache raids. People returned and rebuilt using the sun-dried adobe bricks from within the presidio destroying earlier Spanish buildings. (15)

The name Sabori is connected to Maria Gomez who married Antonio Sabori, son of Don Pedro and Gertrudis Sabori. They lived in this home for many years.

The Old Garrett Stable

private residence

(16) The stable of James Garrett stood at the corner of Tubac Road and the old U.S. Highway Route 89, from Nogales to Tucson.

This adobe building was converted to Tubac's post office and eventually into a residence by the late Mrs. Will Rogers Jr. Mrs. Rogers designed and had built the placita along with the small shrine at the corner of Tubac Road and Burruel Street.

Garrett House

private residence

James T. Garrett Sr. came from Texas in 1913. He was principally a cattleman. He lost his first wife who gave him 5 daughters and his second wife by whom he had 2 boys and a girl. His store and home were in the park just south of the Otero Community Hall. He lost his home and store to the Baca Float No. 3 heirs. (17)

In 1917 Garrett created a sensation by building a two story house with adobe walls. In front of the house, on the new highway, was his new store. By 1926 the U.S. Border Patrol used the store as headquarters.

James T. Garrett Sr. died in 1931.

Will Rogers Jr. and his wife, Collier, came on a visit to Tubac in 1955. They saw two historic buildings that needed repair. Collier decided she wanted the Garrett House which had been used as a hotel and bar.

Tubac Cementery

This appears to be a combination of the English spelling cemetery and the Spanish "cementerio". The piles of rocks on the graves are apparently to protect the graves from coyotes.

Otero Ranch

(19)

The Otero family is one of the original land owners in the Tubac area as Don Toribio Otero was given title to a large tract of land by the King of Spain in 1789. Some of the conditions for accepting the land was that the Oteros were to build a home, plant fruit trees, and start a school.

Manuel Otero, the grandson of Toribio, continued to work the land holding until about 1860. He left Tubac with his family for Sonora, Mexico, to protect them from Apache raids. Manuel died in Mexico in 1863. Four years later his 19 year old son, Sabino, and family returned to Tubac in 1867 and increased the original family land holdings. At one time he was said to have over 75,000 head of cattle and 20 vaqueros. Sabino lived a great deal of his time in Tucson from 1880 to the time of his death in 1914 but still kept active in his Tubac ranch. He was active in the building of the schoolhouse in Tubac in 1885 and restored the family home, "The Hacienda", in 1912.

Teofilo, Sabino's youngest brother, took over the ranch after his brother's death. He was the person responsible for constructing the Otero Hall which took the overflow from the schoolhouse and was used for community events. Teofilo died in 1941.

San Cayentano Del Tumacacori

20

On the east bank of the Santa Cruz River was a village of Pima Indians who were farmers not nomads like the Apaches. When this mission church was built, about 1732, it was located near the Indian community. This church, called San Jose De Tumacacori, was rebuilt several times but construction stopped in 1822 due to lack of funds. It was completely abandoned by 1840.

Franciscan Father Carrillo (died 1795) and Father Gutierrez (died 1821) were the principal builders of this church. They were first buried beneath the sanctuary floor to the left of the altar. In 1935 their remains were transfered to the San Xavier Mission Mortuary Chapel.

The Campo Santo

The Campo Santo - "Holy Field" - was the mission cemetery.

After the mission was abandoned in 1840, the cemetery was used as a corral for cattle. Then along came "pothunters" looting the graves of the Christian Indians.

With the Indian Wars ending, after the surrender of Geronimo, settlers came back to the village of Tumacacori. Although the deteriorating church was still not used, old timers used the sanctified grounds for their dead. The last person buried here was Juanita, an infant, in 1916.

Around the wall are niches for the stations of the cross. The circular building was planned as a mortuary chapel but was never completed. The holes in the walls supported scaffolding for the builders.

21

Introduction to Nogales

A large Mexican land grant was made to Don Jose Elias in 1841. It was known as "Los Nogales De Elias", named for the extensive groves of walnuts growing in the valley.

In 1854 the area became part of the U.S. after the Gadsden Purchase. By 1880, a Jacob Isaacson had opened a trading store on the American side and a Juan Jose Vasquez built a roadhouse on the Mexican side. Both entrepreneurs could see this valley crossing would be popular between the U.S. and western Mexico.

In May 1882 a post office was called Issacson with Jacob as postmaster. Jacob was born in Russia and died in Detroit in 1928. By December 1882 the rail link between the U.S. and Mexico had been completed with the driving in of the "silver spike." The name was then changed from Isaacson to Nogales. By 1893 the municipality was formed after borrowing $2000 from Theodor Gebler, of the new town council, for a seal and operating expenses.

Map No. 6 Nogales

Map Site No.

1. Padre Kino
2. Grande Avenue-Frank Reed School

2a. Cemetery

3. Camp Little
4. 1880 Sculpture
5. Sacred Heart Church

5a. Monseigneur Louis Duval Grave

6. Pimeria Alta Historical Society Museum
7. Overton House (private residence)
8. Ekey House (private residence)
9. Karam House
10. Grant House (private residence)
11. Newsboy
12. Nasib Karam Park
13. Issacson Marker
14. Morley Avenue Pedestrian Border Entrance
15. Santa Cruz County Courthouse

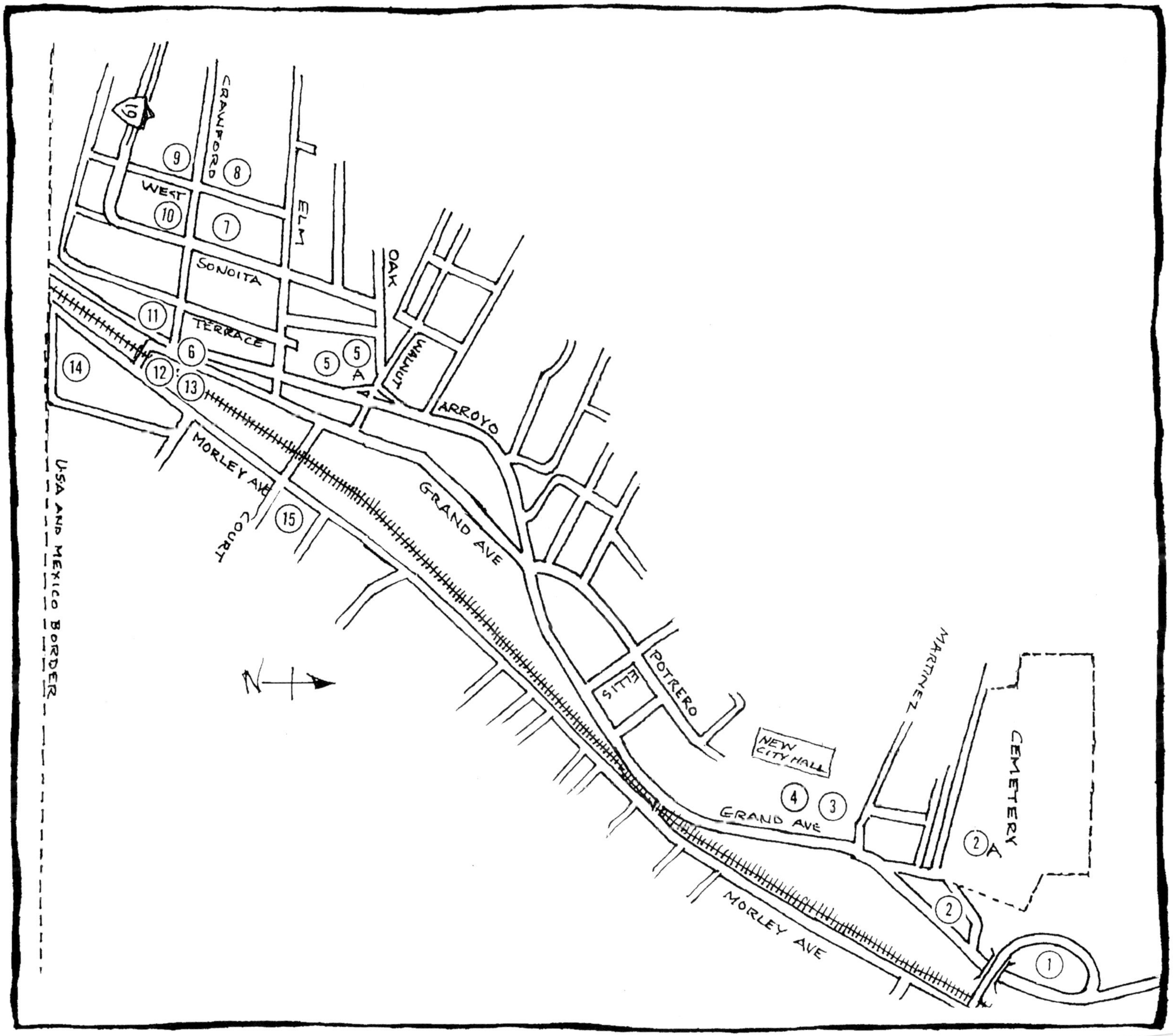

Map No. 6 Nogales

(1)

Padre Kino

This statue is located in a small park that also houses the Chamber of Commerce.

The plaque on the front of the statue reads:

Padre
Eusebio Francisco
Kino S J
Founder of missions
Man of God
Pioneer Explorer
Astronomer
Rancher Teacher
Cartographer
1645-1711

The plaque on the back of the statue reads:

Padre Kino founded 27
missions & vistas. He
made 40 expeditions into
The Pimeria Alta, Baja & California
first visited the village
of Tumacacori in 1691 &
passed this spot many
times enroute to or from
Magdelena where he now rests.

Dedicated, June 11, 1968
Ralph Hamilton Humes, Sculptor
Civic project of the citizens of
Nogales and Santa Cruz County
Erected by the Arizona State Highway Dept.

The statue faces south. On the east side is a relief of San Xavier Mission and on the west it's San Ignacio.

Grande Avenue-Frank Reed School

Grande Avenue 1928 - 1952 Frank Reed School

(2)

Grande Avenue School was founded in 1928 as a grammar school, grades one through eight, for the African American children of Nogales. In 1943 the school's name was changed to Frank A. Reed in honor of a former student, Frank A. Reed, who died in action during World War II. Frank A. Reed School was closed in September 1952 due to desegregation of the Arizona school system.

Teachers were:
Lena Martin (principal) 1928-1952
Florence Mills 1928-1942
Willa Hudson 1942-1943 and 1945-1947
Mildred Simpson Bennett 1944-1945 and 1947-1952

The uniqueness of our school was due to our African and Mexican heritages. Even though segregated, this school turned out some outstanding students that grew up to be the leaders of yesterday, today and tomorrow.

Dedicated Feb. 17, 1996
Pimeria Alta Historical Society
City of Nogales, Arizona

This plaque donated by the Jackson family: Lucius Sr., Angela, Ida, Lucius Jr., David, Arthur, Mary, John, Emma, Eva.

There is no known photograph of this school.

(2) A

The Nogales Cemetery

In 1905 F.F. Granz, Mayor of the town of Nogales, subscribed and made a sworn statement that the public cemetery first occupied this site in 1882.

Knights of Pythias Lodge #13 started occupancy about 1885 as well as the (IOOF) International Order of Odd Fellows and the Masonic Order.

You can drive up the cemetery hill and enter the beautiful tree-lined drive marking the entrance to the grounds. This old but well kept cemetery has many family memorials to the early pioneers and founders of Nogales.

Camp Stephen D. Little

A military camp established in Nogales, Arizona, in November of 1910, was for a generation an integral part of the economic and social life of the community. The post was renamed on December 14, 1915, for Private Little, killed in action during the border troubles which climaxed with the taking of Nogales, Sonora, by revolutionists. After reaching a peak strength of 12,000 in 1914, forces were gradually reduced after World War I to less than 1000 men. The post was abandoned May 5, 1933.

by VFW Santa Cruz Post 2066 and Arizona Historical Society.

③

④

1880

Nogales Centennial Sculpture
presented by
The Nogales Community
October 19, 1980
designed by
Juan Jaime De La Tarre

Sacred Heart Roman Catholic Church of Nogales

5

Founded in January 1887 by the Rev. Father Dolge, then Pastor of Tombstone, who was put in charge as a missionary and visited occasionally. He had a 30- by 22-foot, small adobe church built with a residence attached to the rear. Later Rev. Father Granjon assumed the responsibility of the church.

By 1900, Father Meurer was the first resident priest and he added to the original adobe building.

French-born Rev. Father Duval, from 1905-1915, expanded the church's roll to include school and hospital work. Father Duval was very active in the Tubac church as well.

During the period of 1917 to 1930 the present church took on today's appearance, and by 1946 the church was completely clear of debt.

The bell is found in front of the church, along with the original cornerstone with this inscription:

1910 Ralph M. Parsons
Architect
O.J. Omstead
R.E. Jones, Builders

Rev. H. Granjon
Bishop of Tucson
Rev. L. Duval
Rector

Monsiegneur Louis Duval Grave

(5) A

3 Graves in front of Sacred Heart Church, Nogales

These inscriptions are found on the granite tombstones of the graves on the stone-covered hillside just below the church:

Right Reverend
MSGR Louis Duval
Pastor and Builder
of Sacred Heart Church
Nogales, Arizona
1905-1945
Born in Draguignan, France
May 20, 1864
Ordained in Ferjus, France
June 24, 1888
Died July 14, 1947
R.I.P.

Reverend Father
Terrace Sheridan
Pastor
Sacred Heart Church
Nogales, Arizona
1961-1969
Born in Oldcastle, Ireland
June 21, 1923
Ordained in Carlow, Ireland
June 1, 1947
Died November, 2, 1970
Alleluia

Right Reverend
MSGR Fernand L.
Rouselle
Pastor
Sacred Heart Church
Nogales, Arizona
1945-1954
Born Paris, France
February 10, 1881
Ordained Paris, France
August 21, 1904
Died April 3, 1963
R.I.P.

This marker is found on the same hillside just below the statue:

A Mons Luis Duval
En Conmemoracion De Su
Jubileo De Oro
1888 - Junio 24 - 1938
La Tercera Orden Franciscana

Pimeria Alta Historical Society Museum

6

This stuccoed brick building with a clock tower was built in 1914 by the volunteer fire department and was designed by Henry O. Jaastad. The two story mission style structure was occupied jointly by the city and the fire department until the completion of the new city complex in 1978. Volunteers still occupy the second floor as club rooms.

In 1885 the Nogales Fire Department volunteers were organized. Shortly after, the department purchased a second hand, hand drawn and operated hook and ladder cart, a hose cart, and the pumper known as "Able and Willing" from Tombstone, Arizona.

The pumper served Nogales until 1917. It was retired and is on exhibit at the Pimeria Alta Historical Museum now established in the old Nogales town hall.

The balcony above the door was often used by military officers from Camp Little and town officials to review the troops departing for "somewhere in France" in 1917. Mexican General Alvaro Obregon (soon to become president) also reviewed U.S. troops while he was on an extended U.S. visit.

MUSEUM

Mayor Overton House

private residence

7

The Overton home is a Queen Anne style victorian built 1897-1898.

W.F. Overton was born 1854 in Nevada County, California. He was a Wells Fargo agent in San Francisco who transferred to Tucson in 1885. He became head of the Wells Fargo operations, in Nogales, in 1895. He ran in the mayoral race and won in 1898, with a second term in 1899.

Mayor Overton took a leave of absence from his Wells Fargo job in 1898 to secure a clear patent from the federal government for the Nogales town site. William McKinley was president at the time.

Mayor Overton held the patented tract in trust and began distributing deeds for the lots already surveyed. $5.00 bought the owner his lot but it cost $7.00 to execute the deed.

The Robert Ekey House

private residence

The home was built in 1898. Robert Ekey was an early builder but eventually gave all his attention to mining and cattle raising. His daughter Ada, who became Mrs. Jones, attended Nogales' first public school in 1886. In 1892 she became a teacher herself. Among her pupils was Abelardo Rodriguez who became governor of Sonora and went on to become the president of Mexico during the years 1932-1934. 8

Ada was the county recorder from 1926 to 1932 and was an active historian.

The Karam House

9

This home was built between 1910-1917 of tufa stone and ashlar. It was originally built by Mr. Schuckman who was the local postmaster. Rumor said that Mr. Schuckman pilfered the money apparently to build this house. He commited suicide when discovered.

This then became the Karam home in 1919 and in 1978 became the property of the Santa Cruz County Association for Mentally Retarded Children.

Nasib Karam was a longtime resident of Nogales. He was a prominent lawyer and county attorney and died in 1975. As they had no children, Margarith Elias, his widow, sold the home in 1978.

Jesse Grant House

private residence

(10)

The house was built between 1890 - 1893 and enlarged in 1901 - 1909.

Jesse was the son of Ulysses Simpson Grant (1869-1877), the 18th President. This was his son's legal residence for several years prior to 1907.

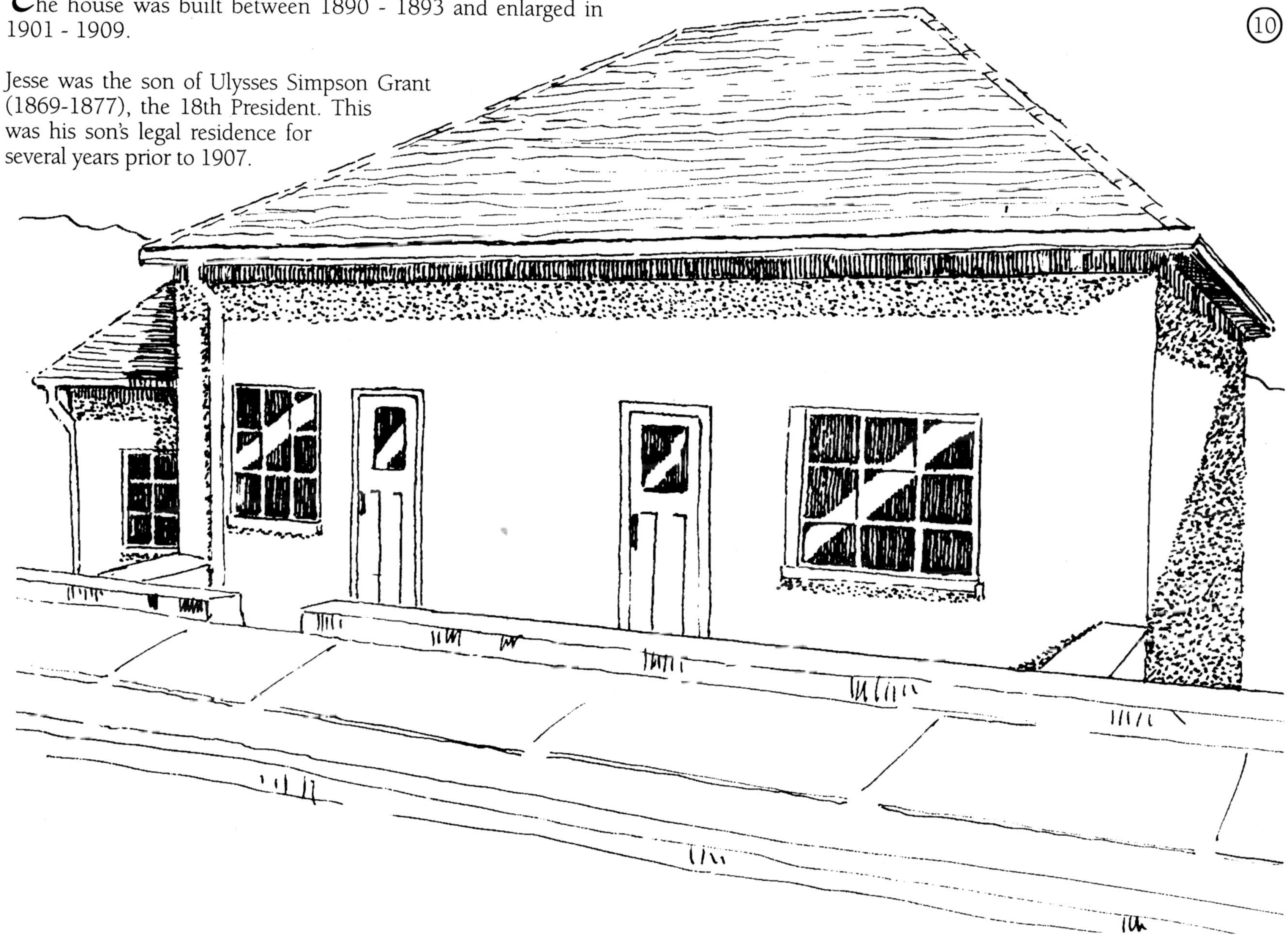

11

Bronze Statue of Newspaper Boy

May 24, 1973
This park is dedicated to
Hanson R. Sisk
Born July 15, 1892
Purchased the Nogales Herald 1920
Died October 23, 1969

The first Nogales newspaper was called the *Frontier* and started publishing in 1885.

From 1885 to 1920 there were several attempts to provide newspaper coverage in Nogales; eg., *El Monitor Fronterio* (Spanish and English), *Nogales News, Daily Reserve, Sunday Herald, Nogales Record, Daily Nogales, Border Vidette, Oasis, and Nogales Times*.

In 1914 the *Nogales Herald* was started. At the same time Hanson Ray Sisk arrived in Nogales from Kentucky as a reporter for the *El Paso Herald* to cover the Mexican Revolution.

Hanson Sisk returned in 1916 to become the business manager for the *Nogales Herald*. He bought the paper in 1920 and remained as publisher until his death in 1969. In 1980 the *Herald* was still being published by the Sisk family.

Nasib Karam Park

(12)

Montezuma Hotel

The Montezuma Hotel, sixty feet east of here, built in 1886, rebuilt twice, and closed in 1965, was the center of Nogales business and social life for more than half a century. The office of owner George Christ, first U.S. customs collector of the Arizona District, was in the building (1890-1893). Important transactions in mining, cattle, and Mexican produce were concluded at the Montezuma and it was a meeting place for notable military & political figures from both sides of the border.

Plaque

Rotary international from citizen's of Nogales
"In Memory Of" those from Santa-Cruz-County
who served and died that the principles of democracy may be preserved

Nogales-Arizona erected June 30, 1949 - World War II
56 men are listed in four columns plus one woman Miss Lona Young

Jacob Isaacson Marker 1880

In Karam Park

In 1880, Jacob Isaacson, the first settler here, set up a trading post close by the spot where this marker sits and Juan Jose Vasquez had a roadhouse on the Sonoran side. A post office called Isaacson, with Jacob as postmaster, was established in 1882. Then, in 1883, Isaacson left the area.

13 Isaacson attended the ceremony when on October 25, 1882, a silver spike was ceremonially driven home by Mrs. William Morley, wife of the Atchison, Topeka and Santa Fe Railways chief engineer who was also general manager of the Sonora Railway Ltd. This marked the meeting place in Nogales where the railways of Mexico and the U.S. met for the first time.

When the Sante Fe Railway built a station in this settlement they called it "Nogales" after the old Mexican rancho. Nogales is a Spanish name meaning walnut; the rancho had groves of walnut trees that grew wild in the valley. Everyone agreed the whole settlement should be called Nogales.

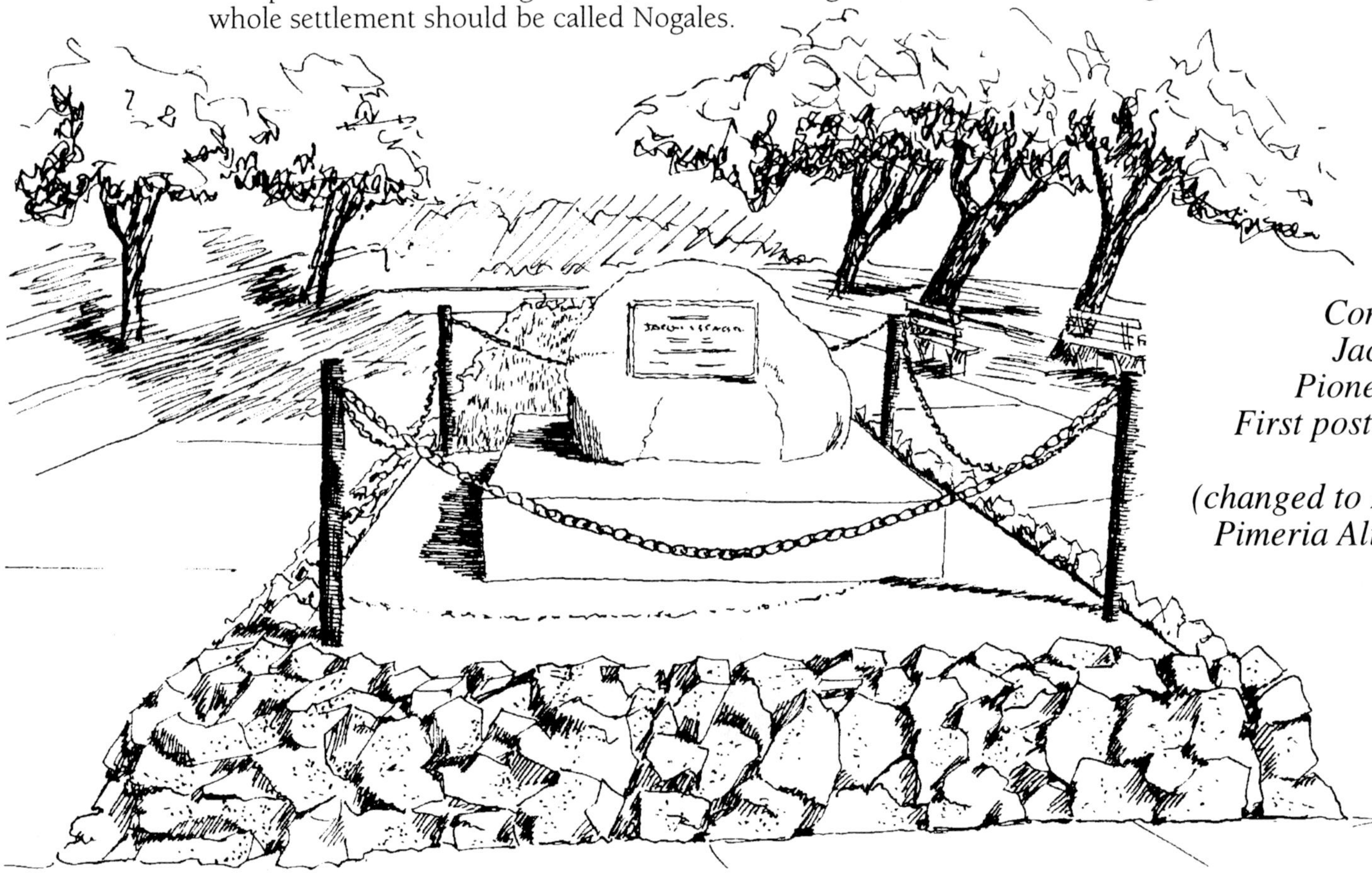

Commemorating
Jacob Isaacson
Pioneer Settler 1880
First postmaster of Isaacson, Arizona
(changed to Nogales June 4, 1883)
Pimeria Alta Historical Society, 1953

Morley Avenue Pedestrian Border Entrance and International Boundary

14

The first garita was built in the early 1920's. Prior to that customs inspectors complained that the business buildings straddle the international boundary line making it almost impossible to enforce custom regulations.

Congress then required all structures be removed from a 60 foot strip along the border.

Revolutions in Mexico didn't help either. In 1918, a U.S. customs officer shot a Mexican border guard who had just killed an American border guard. A day long battle followed after which mutual apologies were made and the border guards, on both sides, were disarmed.

The inspection station was enlarged slightly in 1939 and is in use on Morely Street as a pedestrian entrance today. The main entrance into the U.S. is located at International Street and Grand Avenue. A new and enlarged facility for autos and large trucks, as well as a pedestrian immigration station, was opened in 1995.

In 1853 Lt. William Emory of the United States and Jose Salazar of Mexico led an international survey party hundreds of miles to delineate the boundaries of the Gadsden Purchase. Their first stone survey markers were replaced in 1893 with obelisks such as No.122, sixty feet south of here. Both types of markers were actually ingulfed by early Nogales buildings located in what is now the neutral strip here on International Street.

The plaque is located on the south wall of the building at the corner of International Street and Morley Avenue.

Santa Cruz County Courthouse

(15) This building was designed by Henry Trost who designed many buildings in Tucson. It was completed in 1904 of tufa stone, a limestone quarried within the Nogales city limits. Jail additions were made between 1917 and 1930. Total cost of the building was $35,000 and $4,700 for the cells.

This is the oldest building in continuous use for county government in the state. It was also the first courthouse for Santa Cruz County and was in use for most county business until 1990. The 8-foot statue at the top of the dome is the Goddess of Justice.

In February 1903, 500 people paraded behind a marching band from the Masonic Hall to the new court house. There Judge Williams, using three silver goblets, annointed the corner stone: "The Wheat of Nourishment," "The Wine of Plenty," "The Oil of Joy".

The building is on the National Register of Historic Places.